INFERTILITY

INFERTILITY
Medical, Emotional and Social Considerations

Edited by

Miriam D. Mazor, M.D.

Clinical Instructor in Psychiatry
Harvard Medical School
Boston, MA

Harriet F. Simons, M.S.S.A., L.I.C.S.W.

Doctoral Student, Florence Heller Graduate School
for Advanced Studies in Social Welfare,
Brandeis University, Waltham, MA

HUMAN SCIENCES PRESS, INC.
72 FIFTH AVENUE
NEW YORK, N.Y. 10011

A A Y 9799

Printed in the United States of America
123456789

Library of Congress Cataloging in Publication Data
Main entry under title:

Infertility—medical, emotional, and social
  considerations.

  Bibliography: p.
  Includes index.
  1. Infertility.   2. Infertility—Psychological
aspects.   3. Infertility—Social aspects.   4. Parenthood
—Decision making.   I. Mazor, Miriam D.   II. Simons,
Harriet F.   [DNLM: 1. Infertility.   WP 570 I438]
RC889.I564   1984   616.6'92   83-10872
ISBN 0-89885-140-8
ISBN 0-89885-177-7 (pbk.)

To Racheli and Rafi
M.D.M.

In memory of my mother, Sylvia M. Fishman
H.F.S.

CONTENTS

CONTRIBUTORS

Roberta J. Apfel, M.D. – Assistant Professor of Psychiatry, Harvard Medical School; Associate in Psychiatry, Beth Israel Hospital, Boston, MA.

Stuart B. Bauer, M.D. – Assistant Professor of Surgery (Urology), Harvard Medical School; Assistant in Surgery, Children's Hospital Medical Center, Boston, MA.

Merle J. Berger, M.D., F.A.C.O.G. – Assistant Clinical Professor of Obstetrics and Gynecology, Harvard Medical School, Obstetrician and Gynecologist, Beth Israel Hospital, Boston, MA.

Ann Edwards Boutelle, Ph.D. – Associate Professor of English, Mount Holyoke College, South Hadley, MA.

Ellen K. Bresnick, M.S.W., A.C.S.W., L.I.C.S.W. – Private Practice, Wellesley, MA; Consultant, New England Fertility and Gynecology Associates, Chestnut Hill, MA.

Sharon Gibbons Collotta, R.N., B.S. – Nursing Supervisor, Community Hospital of Newport Richey, Newport Richey, Florida; Former Head Nurse, Fertility, Endocrine and Menopause Clinic, Boston Hospital for Women (now Brigham and Women's Hospital), Boston, MA.

Susan M. Fisher, M.D. – Lecturer and Consultant, University of Chicago, Pritzker School of Medicine, Chicago, Ill.

Harvey W. Freishtat, J.D. – Partner, McDermott, Will and Emery, Boston, MA; Director, Public Responsibility in Medicine and Research

Julie E. Ginsburg, M.S.W., A.C.S.W., L.I.C.S.W. – Director of Adoption Services, Concord Family Service Society, Concord, MA; Former Director, International Adoptions, Newton, MA.

Donald Peter Goldstein, M.D. – Assistant Clinical Professor of Obstetrics and Gynecology, Harvard Medical School; Obstetrician-gynecologist, Brigham and Women's Hospital, Boston, MA; Gynecologist-in-Chief, Children's Hospital Medical Center, Boston, MA.

Stacey Tsairis Kacoyanis, M.S. – Genetic Associate, Prenatal Diagnostic Laboratory, Massachusetts General Hospital, Boston, MA.

Louise Cannon Lazare, R.N., B.S. – Member, Board of Directors, and Past President of the Open Door Society of Mass, Inc., Boston, MA; Administrative Director, Adoption Counselors, Inc., Boston, MA.

Tovah Silver Marion, Ed.D. – Private Practice, Brookline, MA; Formerly Staff and Supervising Psychologist, Walden Clinic, Concord Mental Health Center, Concord, MA.

Miriam D. Mazor, M.D. – Clinical Instructor in Psychiatry, Harvard Medical School; Associate in Psychiatry, Beth Israel Hospital, Boston, MA.

Barbara Eck Menning, R.N., M.P.H. – Founder and Executive Director, RESOLVE, Inc., Belmont, MA. (1973–1982)

Wayne A. Miller, M.D. – Director, Prenatal Diagnostic Laboratory, Massachusetts General Hospital, Boston, MA.

Carol C. Nadelson, M.D. – Professor and Vice Chairman, Tufts University School of Medicine, Department of Psychiatry, and Associate Psychiatrist-in-Chief and Director of Training and Education, Department of Psychiatry, New England Medical Center Hospital, Boston, MA.

Robert A. Newton, M.D. – Assistant Clinical Professor of Urology, Harvard Medical School; Chief of Urology, Newton-Wellesley Hospital, Newton, MA; Consultant in Andrology, Fertility and

Endocrine Clinic, Brigham and Women's Hospital, Boston, MA.

Malkah T. Notman, M.D. – Clinical Professor of Psychiatry, Tufts-New England Medical Center; Lecturer, Harvard Medical School; Psychiatrist, Beth Israel Hospital, Boston, MA.

Alan B. Retik, M.D. – Professor of Surgery (Urology), Harvard Medical School; Chief, Division of Urology, Children's Hospital Medical Center, Boston, MA.

Isaac Schiff, M.D., F.A.C.O.G. – Associate Professor of Obstetrics and Gynecology, Harvard Medical School; Associate Director, Reproductive Endocrinology, Brigham and Women's Hospital, Boston, MA.

Machelle M. Seibel, M.D. – Assistant Professor of Obstetrics and Gynecology, Harvard Medical School; Director, Gyn-Endocrine Laboratory, Beth Israel Hospital, Boston, MA.

Harriet F. Simons, M.S.S.A., L.I.C.S.W. – Doctoral student, Florence Heller Graduate School for Advanced Studies in Social Welfare, Brandeis University, Waltham, MA.

Melvin L. Taymor, M.D., F.A.C.O.G. – Clinical Professor of Obstetrics and Gynecology, Harvard Medical School; Chief, Division of Reproductive Endocrinology, Beth Israel Hospital, Boston, MA.

Irwin E. Thompson, M.D., F.A.C.O.G. – Assistant Clinical Professor of Obstetrics and Gynecology, Harvard Medical School; Obstetrician and Gynecologist, Beth Israel Hospital, Boston, MA.

Sonnet #2 of the "Procreation Sonnets"

When forty winters shall besiege thy brow,
And dig deep trenches in thy beauty's field,
Thy youth's proud livery, so gazed on now,
Will be a tattered weed, of small worth held:
Then being asked where all thy beauty lies,
Where all the treasure of thy lusty days;
To say, within thine own deep sunken eyes,
Were an all-eating shame and thriftless praise.
How much more praise deserved thy beauty's use,
If thou couldst answer— 'This fair child of mine
Shall sum my count, and make my old excuse—'
Proving his beauty by succession thine!
    This were to be new-made when thou art old,
    And see thy blood warm when thou feelst it cold.

—Shakespeare

Cited from; *The Sonnets, Songs and Poems of Shakespeare* edited with Introduction, Running Commentary, Glosses and Notes by Oscar James Campbell. New York: Schocken Books, 1967.

FOREWORD

Miriam D. Mazor

The problem of infertility is as old as human civilization. All cultures, from ancient times to the present, have had their fertility rites and practices, dolls and amulets, herbs and folk medicines to ensure that there would indeed be a new generation to carry on the culture. Traditionally, the woman was held responsible for whether or not offspring were produced, and in most societies the "barren woman" was, and still is, a tragic figure. The woman's worth was perceived largely in terms of childbearing and childrearing abilities; the man had other important roles in the economy and defense of the community. Some notions of the male role in reproduction existed in ancient times, as evidenced by the existence of phallic cults and paraphernalia. However, it was not until the seventeenth century that spermatozoa were observed under the microscope, and not until the eighteenth century that their role in fertilization was discovered. For a while the "homunculus" theory prevailed, which held that a sperm contained a fully formed miniature person, and that the womb provided an incubator in which it could grow. By the nineteenth century, early workers in genetics found that both parents contributed equally to the genetic makeup of the new

individual, except for sex differentiation which is mediated ex-
clusively by the male, and the mammalian ovum was observed.
The twentieth century brought great strides in the understanding of reproductive physiology, the complex events occurring
within the menstrual cycle, and the multiplicity of factors in both
male and female that could enhance or impair conception and
the carriage of a pregnancy to term.

In contemporary America heavy emphasis is placed on self-
fulfillment and self-gratification. We worry about overpopulation and the depletion of our resources. We no longer live in a
culture in which barren wives are cast aside, or men "without
issue" are objects of pity and scorn. The childless adult, whether
single or a partner in a couple, now has social sanction to try out
new life-styles, new roles, and new ways of exploring his or her
own creative potential. Why, then, is infertility a major problem
for so many people today? Why do people subject themselves to
physical, emotional, and financial hardships and privations in
order to achieve parenthood? Social and family pressures not-
withstanding, it is my belief that there is an important push from
within, that parenthood is an integral part of the development
of most adults, and that difficulties or frustrations in attaining
the goal of parenthood have an impact on many aspects of their
lives, their relationships with others, and their own sense of self-
esteem.

Approximately one out of six couples in the United States
has some difficulty in conceiving or carrying a pregnancy to
term.[1] According to the American Fertility Society, a marriage is
considered barren or infertile when a successful pregnancy,
leading to a live birth, has not occurred within a year of regular
sexual relations without contraception. Within that period,
about 80 percent of sexually active couples will conceive; in a
second year perhaps as many as 15 percent will conceive. During
the third year a smaller group will conceive, resulting in an overall inclusive accumulative percentage of 9 percent for the second
and third years. The remainder have an infertility problem, with
their chances for conceiving decreasing over time in the absence
of treatment. Although exact figures are impossible to obtain,
tentative findings suggest that there has been an increase in the

infertile population in recent years. Both men and women are maximally fertile in their mid-twenties. Postponement of marriage and childbearing into the thirties and forties, for a variety of personal, social, and economic reasons, contributes to the number of people who have or will have an infertility problem. A small but growing number of individuals is seeking reversal of voluntary sterilization as their life circumstances and goals change. As the prevalence of veneral disease rises, so does the incidence of reproductive tract scarring that may potentially cause infertility in both men and women who have not obtained treatment early enough. Infertility may result from the use of certain contraceptive methods; for example, the IUD (intrauterine device) may cause infection and scarring of the Fallopian tubes, or contraceptive pills may lead to problems in ovulation after their use is discontinued, especially in women who have prior histories of irregular menses.

Endometriosis, the occurrence of endometrial tissue outside of the uterine cavity, is another significant cause of infertility. With each cycle, the extrauterine tissue bleeds and sheds, and may cause pain, scarring, and cyst formation, depending on its location. This condition affects approximately 1/4 to 1/3 of infertile women and becomes more disabling with each menstrual cycle. Therapeutic abortions may, even in the absence of infection, cause damage to the cervix and the inability to carry a later, desired pregnancy to term.

Other factors include exposure to various drugs, chemicals, and radiation, which may affect fertility, and whose results may not be evident until many years later (e.g., people exposed to DES, diethylstilbestrol, *in utero*, often have reproductive tract abnormalities that may not be recognized until they reach adulthood [chapters 16 and 17]).

In addition to the actual increase in the infertile population, there is an apparent increase as well. The subject is less "taboo" than in former years. Although in the vast majority of cases, infertility is not caused by problems of sexual function, the traditional association of sex and reproduction made the subject seem shameful or embarrassing. As it has become acceptable to discuss sexual matters more freely, it has become easier to acknowledge infertility. Recent advances in diagnostic and treatment possibilities offer greater hope to the infertile couple, so that there is a real impetus to pursue the problem more aggressively. The general public is now better informed, and people expect and demand treatment for medical problems. Another significant push toward recognition and treatment of the problem comes from the fact that there are relatively few infants available for adoption. The relative ease of obtaining therapeutic abortions, coupled with the tendency of unwed mothers to keep their babies, has made adoption a difficult project, requiring an enormous investment of time, energy, and money, Adoption is no longer the easy alternative it was once thought to be. Furthermore, it should be noted that adoption is not a cure for infertility, but is an alternative method of building a family. Although everyone knows about a couple who adopted a baby and the wife immediately became pregnant, infertile couples who do and do not adopt actually conceive at about the same rate.[2]

Demographers, sociologists, social workers, and public health workers are becoming more interested in the problem of infertility. Westoff[3] points out that in this century the trend in industrialized Western countries is toward a declining birthrate, despite an occasional reversal like the Baby Boom following World War II. The birthrates in these countries may well fall below the optimal Zero Population Growth level. In that event, a negative growth rate, or growth based on immigration rather than birthrate, may well carry social and economic problems. In countries such as Sweden, the government has already begun to foster a pronatalist policy, including economic bonuses for having children and prolonged maternity and paternity leaves from work. It may become a matter of national interest in most of the developed countries to initiate programs for the treatment and prevention of infertility as part of family planning programs to encourage the birth of *wanted* children.

The focus of this book will be on the psychological and emotional aspects of the infertility experience. It will present various perspectives on infertility from professionals in different disciplines, as well as some experiential accounts. It is the outgrowth of a workshop, *Medical and Psychiatric Aspects of Infertility,* presented at Beth Israel Hospital, Boston, Massachussetts, on October 13 to 14, 1978, whose aim was to foster discussion and exchange, rather than to arrive at a consensus. It is not intended as a textbook in the usual sense of the word, but is rather a presentation of ideas and opinions about the current state of knowledge in the field. A diversity of approaches and terminologies of different disciplines are represented, and at times there may be disagreement about a particular issue.

The reader interested in an overview of infertility addressed to the general public would do well to read Menning's book on infertility.[1] Taymor's text is written for medical students and physicians, and presents the issues clearly and concisely, with excellent diagrams and bibliography.[4] Behrman and Kistner offer the specialist detailed and comprehensive information and references,[5] as do Amelar, Dubin, and Walsh in their work on male infertility.[6]

REFERENCES

1. Menning, B.E. *Infertility: a guide for the childless couple.* New Jersey: Prentice-Hall, 1977.

2. Arronet, G. Bergquist, C., & Parehl, M. The influence of adoption on subsequent pregnancy in infertile marriages. *International Journal of Fertility.* 19(3):159–162, March 1974.

3. Westoff, C.F. Marriage and fertility in the developed countries. *Scientific American, 239*(6); 51–57, December 1978.

4. Taymor, M.L. *Infertility.* New York: Grune and Stratton, 1978.

5. Behrman, S.J., & Kistner, R.S. (Eds.). *Progress in infertility.* Boston: Little, Brown and Co., 1975.

6. Amelar, R., D. Dubin, L., & Walsh, P.C., *Male infertility.* Philadelphia: Saunders, 1977.

Part I

MEDICAL, EMOTIONAL, AND SOCIAL ISSUES

Chapter 1

THE MEDICAL WORKUP
Female and Combined Problems

Irwin E. Thompson

Infertility is a relative term implying a lack of fertility, or the inability to produce a live child. The definition proposed by the American Fertility Society has been widely accepted and states that, "A marriage is to be considered barren after a year of coitus without contraception."

Fecundability, the capacity of any couple to conceive, is influenced by four demographic correlations—the age of the woman, the age of the man, frequency of intercourse, and duration of coital exposure. Fertility in both the male and female appears to be maximal around 24 to 25 years. Furthermore, it has been shown that the proportion of conceptions achieved in less than six months rises with the frequency of intercourse, while it has also been shown that approximately 63 percent of fertile couples will achieve conception with six months of exposure and 80 percent in one year.

The management of an infertility problem should incorporate four major principles: 1) the diagnosis of any given couple as being infertile, 2) consideration of the couple as an entity, 3) evaluation of the probable factors involved, 4) awareness of

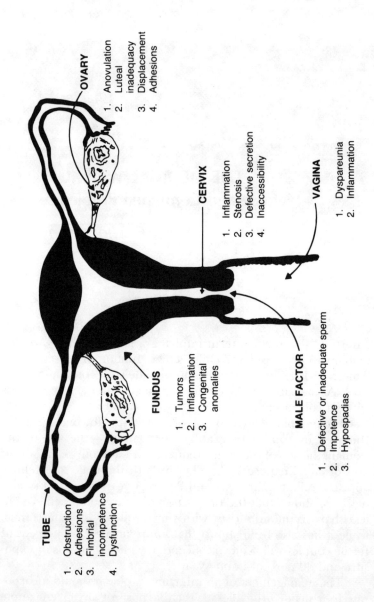

TUBE

1. Obstruction
2. Adhesions
3. Fimbrial incompetence
4. Dysfunction

OVARY

1. Anovulation
2. Luteal inadequacy
3. Displacement
4. Adhesions

CERVIX

1. Inflammation
2. Stenosis
3. Defective secretion
4. Inaccessibility

FUNDUS

1. Tumors
2. Inflammation
3. Congenital anomalies

VAGINA

1. Dyspareunia
2. Inflammation

MALE FACTOR

1. Defective or inadequate sperm
2. Impotence
3. Hypospadias

Figure 1. Causes of Infertility.

emotional factors and potential problems precipitated by the investigative process itself.

In most cases therefore, investigation should probably not be initiated until after at least twelve months of attempted conception. Obviously, there will be exceptions to this guideline.

It is important psychologically and medically that the couple be considered as an entity and that both parties be involved in the diagnostic process. It is helpful also to meet with both from time to time during the investigation and to discuss all findings to date.

The first visit, normally, should involve both partners and provide an opportunity to discuss the requirements for the basic infertility investigation. These requirements are based on functional and anatomic considerations of the causes of infertility. Infertility can be attributed totally or partially to male causes in 40 percent of cases. In the female, approximately 30 percent of infertility is due to tubal causes, 20 percent to ovarian causes, 15 percent to cervical causes. The remainder can be attributed to other causes, or undiagnosed causes.

Five Basic Tests

In addition to the general physical exam of each partner, there are five basic tests, which will help define the general area that will require further investigation or treatment.

1. *Semen analysis* of the male should be performed early in the course of the investigation, since evaluation of this factor is usually simpler than the sum of the factors in the female. The sample is usually produced by masturbation after several days of abstention and should be evaluated as soon as possible after collection.

A normal semen analysis can only be broadly defined in terms of the usual parameters associated with fertility. Thus a "normal" semen analysis may be defined as one that shows at least 20 million sperm per milliliter (ml), but usually more than 35 million per ml, a semen volume of 2 to 5 ml, sperm motility of greater than 60 percent with normal progression and at least 60

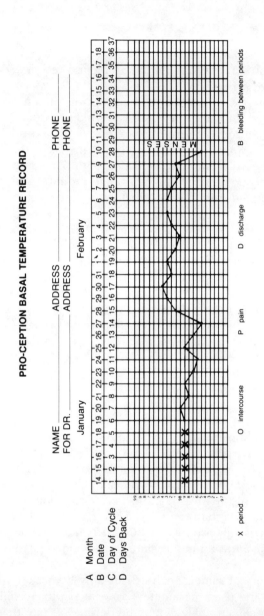

Figure 2. Typical Ovulatory Basal Temp. Chart.

percent normal morphology (shape and size). In any patient the sperm count may vary from ejaculate to ejaculate by about 20 percent.

2. Evaluation of the ovulatory factor is initiated by the use of *basal body temperature* (BBT) recordings (taken immediately on arising in the morning) and verified by timed endometrial biopsy. Presumption of normal ovulation may be made from a typical BBT chart.

A biphasic curve in which the basal temperatures of the last 12 to 15 days of the cycle (the luteal phase) demonstrate a sustained rise 0.3 to 1 degree F higher than those of the first half of the cycle (the follicular phase) is almost certain evidence of ovulation. The temperature change is a thermal response to progesterone production and is believed to occur when the circulating progesterone level reaches approximately 2 ng per ml. As is well known, however, the timing of the actual occurrence of ovulation remains somewhat in dispute. Since progesterone production by the follicle actually increases prior to ovulation, it seem likely that the thermal shift bears a variable relationship to ovulation certainly in different patients and probably in the same patient from cycle to cycle.

BBTs are therefore also of assistance in diagnosing anovulatory bleeding and in situations of the inadequate luteal phase, when the normal pattern is not observed. In anovulatory cycles, there is no recognizable "thermal shift" whatsoever (Figure 3).

Endometrial biopsy is usually a sine qua non for the substantiation of the diagnosis of any of the situations outlined, the diagnosis, of course, being based on the presence or absence of an adequate or inadequate progestational effect on the endometrium, during the second half of the cycle.

The occurrence of ovulation represents the midpoint of the complicated sequential changes that take place during the normal menstrual cycle. These changes occur in many different organs, including hypothalamic production of luteinizing hormone releasing hormone (LH–RH), pituitary secretion of gonadotropins, and ovarian production of estrogens. After ovulation, the corpus luteum is formed, producing the typical pattern of increased progesterone secretion in the luteal phase. The

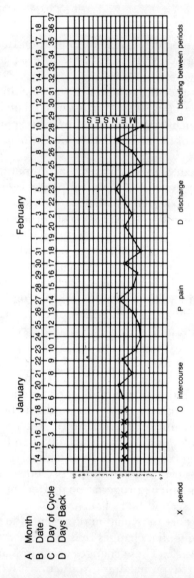

Figure 3. Typical Anovulatory Basal Temp. Chart.

8

quality of corpus luteum function may be assessed by direct measurement of circulating progesterone or by endometrial biopsy, as already mentioned.

In patients who are not ovulating, induction of ovulation is frequently successfully achieved by specific therapy. Clomiphene citrate is the most commonly used agent, which can achieve a 70 to 80 percent ovulatory rate in appropriate patients.[1] Patients who do not respond to clomiphene may be treated with human menopausal gonadotropin injections (Pergonal), and again a 70 to 80 percent ovulatory rate can be achieved in this group. For the relatively small group who do not ovulate because of hyperprolactinemia, (a condition in which the pituitary produces too much prolactin), bromoergocryptine is the therapy of choice.

The *post-coital* test is performed one to two days prior to ovulation. This test allows for evaluation of the formation of good cervical mucus with signs of adequate estrogenization of the mucus, namely ferning of the mucus with increased elasticity (spinnbarkeit). Given proper timing of the test, the number of active sperm found in the mucus 10 to 16 hours after coitus may be correlated with the occurrence of pregnancy. Ten or more active sperm per microscopic high power field is evidence of adequate insemination, while less than five active sperm is considered a poor post-coital test. In a series of 569 patients, Taymor showed a significant correlation between good and bad tests and subsequent occurrence of pregnancy.[2]

The importance of the post-coital test is related to the fact that immunological factors may actually cause infertility.[2] That is, in 10 to 15 percent of cases, the female may develop antibodies to her partner's sperm, so that the sperm are immobilized by an antigen-antibody reaction. This type of problem can be detected by the post-coital test or by in vitro techniques measuring sperm mobility in the cervical mucus. Treatment of this problem is controversial, since no therapeutic modality has been shown to be unequivocally effective. Fortunately, a number of couples do conceive despite the presence of the sperm antibodies existing in the female.

Tubal patency may be tested with either tubal insufflation with carbon dioxide (Rubin's Test) or intrauterine injection of radio-opaque dye (hysterosalpingography, HSG). The Rubin's test is of limited value and should be used only as an early screening test. Most patients will require HSG for adequate evaluation of the uterus and for verification of tubal patency. HSG should be performed in the follicular phase of the cycle and may occasionally have a therapeutic effect in addition to its diagnostic usefulness.

In patients with problems of tubal obstruction, corrective surgery is frequently attempted. Successful pregnancy following surgery depends on the type of tubal defect present and the magnitude of surgery involved. The success rate is approximately 40 to 50 percent, although it is hoped that the recent introduction of tubal microsurgery techniques will improve this figure.

A minor surgical procedure, *laparoscopy*, is useful for visualization of the pelvic organs. It is frequently indicated for diagnosis of endometriosis (presence of endometrial tissue outside the uterine cavity), adhesions (scars) due to a variety of causes, and other structural abnormalities.

In vitro fertilization and implantation of the blastocyst into the uterus has recently been accomplished in patients with otherwise hopeless tubal impairment and offers another approach to this type of problem. Numerous difficulties are associated with these techniques, however, and it is unlikely that they will be readily or easily available in the immediate future. (See Chapter 21).

Further management of the couple will depend on whether the cause of infertility has been identified and what form of therapy appears necessary. The diagnostic approach outlined will normally lead to further investigation of any one of the primary problems where delineated, namely male factor problems, or in the female, vaginal, or cervical causes, uterine causes, tubal causes, or ovarian causes, including other endocrine problems affecting ovulation.

At all times discussion of the problems and of possible therapies with both partners will help reduce emotional stress and

the negative psychological impact of the evaluation. It is emphasized that infertility may severely affect the emotional well-being
of the couple, and the physician must keep this aspect of the
problem in mind at all times. Some form of infertility counseling
or support group is helpful to many couples, and each couple
investigated should be made aware of these options.

REFERENCES

1. Behrman, S.J., Kistner, R.S., (Eds.). *Progress in infertility.* Boston: Little, Brown and Co., 1975.

2. Taymor, M.L. *Infertility.* New York: Grune and Stratton, 1978.

Chapter 2

THE MEDICAL WORKUP
Male Problems

Robert A. Newton

For many years problems relating to male infertility were thought to be untreatable. This is no longer thought to be so. In recent years there have been many advances in the diagnosis and treatment of male infertility problems, and much can be done where male factors are involved in a couple's infertility. On the other hand, it should also be pointed out that much of the current therapy for men with an infertility problem is empirical and is not based on a complete understanding of the pathophysiology involved.

About 20 percent of presumably fertile males undergoing vasectomy have sperm counts below 20 million/ml. (the lower limit of normal). Since 20 percent of men with counts below this level achieve pregnancy without therapy, results of therapy must be viewed against this figure unless we are talking about azoospermia (no sperm in the ejaculate).

Another point to be remembered is the fact that infertility is a problem of the couple and not specifically a female or male factor problem. This is very important in assessing a couple's infertility state because it demands that both the husband and wife should have a complete evaluation simultaneously. Very frequently numerous factors are involved, both male and female, and thus to withhold investigation of one partner because there is an obvious problem in the other is to be avoided.

Furthermore, in the evaluation of male infertility, it should be remembered that semen quality may vary considerably from time to time. In order to establish a reliable baseline of semen quality, multiple semen analyses should be performed, preferably at laboratories specifically interested in doing semen analyses. There might be exceptions to this general rule in situations of azoospermia or in very obviously normal specimens. Although at the present time we do not understand the effect of psychological factors on semen quality, they probably do play a role. For example, a patient whose high-pressured, anxiety-producing job as a hockey coach reduced his semen quality to a subfertile level each year during the hockey season (with the expected three month delay in appearance of reduced semen quality), had considerably better semen quality during the summer.

The causes of male infertility have been divided below into eight categories.

I. OBSTRUCTION

Obstruction in the vas deferens or in the epidydimis (the latter is much more common as a naturally occurring event) is a treatable form of male infertility. Dr. Robert Schoysman of Belgium thinks that as many as 25 percent of all infertile males have some degree of obstruction as a cause of their infertility.[1] Obstruction may cause not only azoospermia, but severe oligospermia (low sperm count) in some cases. Operations using the surgical microscope have brought a great deal of encouragement for the possibility of correcting obstructive causes of infertility. Various types of congenital and acquired defects may cause obstruction, and some of these may be amenable to surgical correction. The absence of infection in these cases often leads to better surgical results.

Obstruction resulting from infection, particularly if it is the result of an old, untreated infection, is very difficult to treat.

Antibiotic therapy is often ineffective if the infection is old and the obstruction is due to scarring. Surgical intervention frequently gives poor results. We have a long way to go in identifying the specific organisms that are involved in obstructive disease of the reproductive tract. It has recently been found that Chlamydia may be a cause of spontaneous epidydimitis in the age group below 35.[2] On the other hand, Mycoplasma may not be as common a cause of epidydimal infection as was previously thought.

Prior surgery, such as hernia repairs, in which the vas deferens has been accidentally divided, either bilaterally or unilaterally, is another cause of obstruction. Surgical therapy yields poor results in these cases because of the atrophy of the vas deferens that frequently seems to follow; especially when the repair was done in childhood.

In the instance of surgical correction of obstruction due to vasectomy, a much greater degree of success has been obtained using the surgical microscope. Vasovasotomies are now quite feasible and give good results. There is close to 90 percent success in getting sperm in sufficient numbers into the ejaculate. Pregnancy rates have been in the 50 to 70 percent range, as would be expected with this quality of semen.[3] However, the success rate is dependent on finding sufficient numbers of viable sperm at the proximal end of the vas deferens at the time of the operation. In addition the success rate of this type of surgery depends on the length of time the vasectomy has been in effect, and whether or not there was rupture of the epidydimal duct.

II. VARICOCELE

A big breakthrough in male infertility problems has been the discovery that a varicocele (varicose veins in the scrotum), even though unilateral (it is most common on the left side), may be a cause of infertility. Although some series have been biased in their numbers, perhaps as many as 25 percent of all male infertility cases are caused by a varicocele. A unilateral varicocele may be the cause of progressive severe oligospermia, even azoospermia, because the cross-circulation in the scrotum allows the varicocele to affect both testes. There have been some striking improvements in semen quality following ligation of the spermatic vein, and a significant pregnancy rate of between 35 and 40 percent.[4] The exact pathophysiology involved in the production of poor semen quality in the presence of varicocele has so far eluded us. Excessive heat in the scrotum due to the enlarged veins and poor circulation of androgens and other hormones via the incompetent spermatic vein are theoretical causes for the decreased spermatogenesis, but these theories have not been borne out by clinical studies. More recent studies have suggested that the varicocele may impair semen quality by affecting those cells not directly producing sperm (e.g., Leydig cells, and Sertoli cells).

As is true with other therapies, the selection of patients who will respond to spermatic vein ligation is the crucial problem. Dr. John MacLeod at Cornell University Medical College was the first to describe the entity known as "stress effect" in semen analyses.[5] This consists of a lowered count, decrease in motility and forward progression of sperm, and the appearance of immature forms in the ejaculate. This "stress effect" is not specific for varicocele, but has helped considerably in the selection of patients who might respond to the operation.

III. CHROMOSOMAL DEFECTS

A third cause of male infertility is chromosomal defects. These are not amenable to therapy at the present time. Such entities as Klinefelter's syndrome, Reifenstein's syndrome, Kallman's syndrome and cystic fibrosis are cases in point. Whether or not spermatogenic arrest, and Sertoli-cell-only syndrome are chromosomal defects or are due to some other, treatable cause is yet to be determined. Another cause of primary testicular failure is the undescended testis. It is commonly thought that a unilateral undescended testis does not result in infertility if the contralateral testis is normally descended. However, recent studies suggest that there may be primary testicular failure in the supposedly normal testis.[6] In any event, primary testicular failure as a cause of male infertility is a discouraging entity with very little available in the way of successful therapy.

IV. INFECTION

Infection as a cause of infertility is a controversial subject. I think there must be some cases in which infection does play a significant role. However, as I have previously indicated, specific identification of the organisms involved is difficult, and treatment of the end results of infection, where obstruction is involved, is unrewarding. If infection is the cause of poor motility, appropriate antibiotic therapy should more effective. Whether or not this is true is a matter of current debate. E. coli has been shown, in vitro, in concentrations of 10^6 per milliliter (ml.) to cause a significant drop in the percentage of motile sperm, to about 40 percent, and there also appears to be some agglutination or clumping of sperm.[7] Mycoplasma and Chlamydia have also been implicated as causes of poor sperm motility. Longevity of motility in sperm may also be affected, and for this reason it is important that semen analyses record motility not only when the specimen is brought to the laboratory, but more important two, three, or even six hours after ejaculation. One can be woefully misled by good motility at one hour, the time that motility studies are carried out in most laboratories.

Assumptions that vaginal mycoplasma may come in contact with sperm seem doubtful as a factor in male infertility. However, electron microscopic studies of spermatozoa that have been mixed with T-mycoplasma are impressive in that they show a sticky substance that literally ties the spermatozoan tail in knots.[8] Chlamydia may be a more likely cause of infertility because these organisms have been cultured from the epidydimis, and this is where we find most of the problems relating to obstruction.

Infection probably also has some effect on glandular function of the accessory glands and may also bring about an immunological response to the individual's sperm because of disruption of the genital tract.

V. Auto-Immune Responses

There has been a great deal of discussion about the role of auto-immune responses in male infertility. To date, however, no relationship between the presence of sperm antibodies in a man, and infertility, has been conclusively demonstrated. Furthermore, no adequate treatment for the presence of sperm antibodies has been developed. The use of very high doses of cortisone, specifically Medrol 96 mg. per day for seven days, may be therapeutic in reducing the antibody titer and has given encouraging results.[9] This suggests that auto-immune responses may play some role in male infertility. The presence of sperm antibodies in men is possible because spermatogenesis takes place within the blood/testis barrier and, therefore, the adult individual does not recognize his own sperm as self. Accordingly, when spermatozoa enter adult tissues either from operative procedures (e.g., vasectomy) or from injury to the genital tract from infectious processes, the individual produces antibodies to his own sperm. These antibodies cause agglutination and immobilization of sperm, and, indeed, these factors have been observed in semen specimens in the presence of sperm antibodies.

VI. Endocrine Defects

Another cause of male infertility is specific endocrine defects. There are patients with hypogonadotropic hypogonadism who may be made fertile by replacing the missing or diminished gonadotropins.

Another group of patients with endocrine defects are those with adrenogenital syndrome who may be subfertile. These patients produce excessive adrenal androgens which then suppress spermatogenesis. These patients can be treated successfully with Prednisone.

Recently, with the advent of better methods for detecting hyperprolactinemia, it has been found that prolactin adenomas are a definite cause of impotence and loss of libido in men.

This can be treated successfully with Bromocriptine therapy. It is not clear just what role hyperprolactinemia may play in male infertility; possibly the excess prolactin interferes with the proper utilization of testosterone and thereby results in oligospermia.

VII. Idiopathic Oligospermia and Asthenospermia

A large group of male patients with subfertility fall under this category. As we are better able to define specific causes for infertility, this category will become smaller. Unfortunately, at present it comprises the bulk of patients with subfertility. Treatment has been strictly empirical and not very successful. The use of pituitary gonadotropins (HCG and HMG) has been tried in oligospermic men without much success. In a summary of results from a number of andrologic centers, Rosemberg reported that the percentage of men whose sperm counts improved with gonadotropin therapy, and the pregnancy rates, were very similar to untreated patients in a fertility clinic.[10] This was true even when the patients were divided into two groups—those whose oligospermia was severe (less than 10 million per cc.) or moderate (10 to 20 million per cc.). There is no statistical proof of a therapeutic effect from empirical gonadotropin therapy in idiopathic oligospermia.

Another form of empirical treatment for idiopathic oligospermia which has been used extensively in the past is testosterone rebound therapy. Heller et al., in 1950 and again in 1972 demonstrated some success with this form of therapy,[11] although most investigators have not been able to reproduce the results that Heller obtained. The improvement in semen quality obtained after a course of testosterone treatment appears to be short-lived, and it is unlikely that many couples would achieve a pregnancy in so short a period of semen quality improvement.

Low dose androgen therapy, using either Mesterolone or Fluoxymesterone has been tried, but with little success.

More recently Clomiphene Citrate has been used in patients

with idiopathic oligospermia. Encouraging results were reported by Paulsen and Waksman in 1976,[12] but the difficulty with this form of treatment is that there is no way to select those patients who are likely to respond to Clomiphene.[13]

VIII. Miscellaneous

Finally there is a group of patients with infertility whom I have classified as a "miscellaneous" category. These are patients who have a variety of defects that seem to play a role in their subfertility.

It is well known that in most men the first portion of the ejaculate contains the best specimen, both in terms of numbers of sperm and quality and percentage of motility. By using a split-ejaculate obtained either by a withdrawal intercourse technique, or, less successfully, by using the first portion of semen for artificial insemination, pregnancies have resulted. It is difficult to explain why this is so. In patients who have a large volume of semen there may be a toxic factor responsible for the production of such a large volume of semen, and this factor may be present in higher quantities in the second portion of the ejaculate. This seems reasonable in view of the fact that ejaculation is a sequential process, with sperm ejaculated first, followed by prostatic fluid, and finally, seminal vesicular fluid.

Another group of patients are those who produce a very viscous semen. The use of Alevaire as a douche in the woman prior to intercourse to break down the viscosity has resulted in pregnancies in several instances. It should be noted that Alevaire has the same pH as semen and therefore does not appear to harm spermatozoa.

There are many drugs that may affect fertility. The best known are Myleran (used in the treatment of leukemia) and other alkylating agents such as TEM and Chlorambucil (used in the treatment of malignant lymphoma); these drugs can cause azoospermia. Cyclophosphamide (used to treat rheumatoid arthritis, nephrotic syndrome, and glomerulonephritis) has been shown to cause severe oligospermia or azoospermia. Methotrexate (often used for treatment of psoriasis) may do the same. Colchicine may cause azoospermia in some individuals, but the effect appears to be reversible. Dilantin (an antiepileptic drug) has been shown to depress both FSH (Follicle Stimulating Hormone) levels and spermatogenesis. High doses of aspirin may cause inhibition of prostaglandin E and F and may result in unexplained infertility. Individuals exposed to DES in utero may have anatomic abnormalities and abnormal semen analyses, as will be discussed in Chapter 16.

Marijuana has been shown to cause chromosome damage when used more than once a week. Its effect on testicular tissue is similar to that of DDT. Nitrofurantoin (an antimicrobial agent used for certain urinary tract infections) has been shown to cause depression in spermatogenesis by interfering with carbohydrate metabolism in the germinal epithelium. It produces an arrest at the primary spermatocyte stage. Monoamine oxidase inhibitors (a class of antidepressant) cause azoospermia or severe oligospermia.

Radiation can certainly suppress spermatogenesis, but has been shown to be reversible with time in some cases.

Retrograde ejaculation, i.e., flow of semen backwards into the bladder obviously results in infertility. It is difficult, but not impossible, to obtain viable sperm from bladder urine in order to produce a pregnancy.

Other toxic drugs, such as industrial chemicals, fertilizers, and herbicides, may result in infertility, but to date a causal relationship has been proven for only a very few.

This has been a short review of the causes of male infertility, their diagnoses, and treatment. The discovery of infertility can be psychologically devastating. Treatment of the infertile male has been improving and offers encouragement to many of those patients to whom we have had little to offer in the past.

REFERENCES

1. Schoysman, R. 9th World Cong. of Fertility and Sterility, Miami Beach, Fla., April 12, 1977. Personal communication.

2. Berger, R., et al. Chlamydia trachomatis as a cause of acute "idiopatic epididymitis". *New England Journal of Medicine, 298* (30), 1978.

3. Silber, S. Vasectomy and vasectomy reversal. *Fertility & Sterility, 29* (125), 1978.

4. Newton, R. et al. The effect of varicocelectomy on sperm count, motility, and conception rate. *Fertility & Sterility, 34* (250), 1980.

5. MacLeod, J. Seminal cytology in the presence of varicocele. *Fertility & Sterility, 16* (735), 1965.

6. Lipschultz, L., et al. Testicular function after orchiopexy for unilaterally undescended testis. *New England Journal of Medicine, 295* (15–18), 1976.

7. Del Porto, G., et al. Bacterial effect on sperm motility. *Urology V, No. 5* (638), 1975.

8. Fowlkes, D. et al. Evidence by scanning electron microscopy for an association between spermatozoa and T-mycoplasma in men of infertile marriage. *Fertility & Sterility, 26* (1203), 1975.

9. Hendry, W., et al. The results of intermittent high dose steroid therapy for male infertility due to antisperm antibodies. *Fertility & Sterility, 36* (351), 1981.

10. Rosemberg, E. Medical treatment of male infertility. *Andrologia* (Suppl.), *1* (95), 1976.

11. Rowley, M., Heller, C. The testosterone rebound phenomenon in the treatment of male infertility. *Fertility & Sterility, 23* (490), 1972.

12. Paulson, D., Wackzman, J. Clomiphene citrate in the management of male infertility. *Journal of Urology, 115* (73), 1976.

13. Epstein, J. Clomiphene treatment in oligospermic infertile males. *Fertility & Sterility, 28* (741), 1977.

14. Amelar, R., Dubin, L., & Walsh, P. *Male infertility.* Philadelphia: W. B. Saunders Co., 1977, p. 92.

Chapter 3

EMOTIONAL REACTIONS TO INFERTILITY*

Miriam D. Mazor

For a long time, the subject of infertility has been rather neglected in the psychiatric literature or has been treated in a manner that has lagged far behind our medical understanding of the problem. The focus of this paper will be on reactions to infertility as a developmental crisis in adult life, but I would like to digress for a moment and discuss the issue of psychiatric factors as a *cause* of infertility.

Two decades ago psychogenic factors were thought to be causative in about 30 to 40 percent of all infertile couples. The diagnosis of what was then called "functional" or "psychogenic" infertility was made largely by exclusion—i.e., the absence of demonstrable organic pathology. Elaborate theories about the personalities and psychodynamics of these patients were formulated and then treated as facts, with psychotherapy directed toward a working-through of the presumed conflicts in order to

---

*This paper was presented at the 133rd Annual Meeting of the American Psychiatric Association, in San Francisco, on May 7, 1980, as part of a Symposium (#43) on Emotional Aspects of Problems in Reproduction.

achieve a pregnancy. Attempts to confirm these hypotheses, based on psychiatric interviews and psychological tests, were either inconclusive or irreproducible; an excellent review of the literature is presented in Denber's article.[1]

With the development of improved diagnostic techniques and a better understanding of reproductive physiology, a diagnosis can now be established for over 90 percent of infertile couples; through treatment, about half of these can be helped to achieve a pregnancy. The term "normal infertile couple," which is sometimes seen in the medical literature, is as misleading in its own way as the term "psychogenic" or "functional" infertility, for it implies that *no* cause exists for the problem. The term "unexplained" infertility seems preferable in that it honestly admits to current limitations in our diagnostic skills.

Drake and Tredway[2] studied couples evaluated for infertility using procedures standard in 1972 and were able to demonstrate organic pathology in all but 10 percent. When the female partners of the undiagnosed 10 percent underwent laparoscopy, then a relatively new procedure, a high proportion of these women had unsuspected endometriosis, with peritubal and ovarian adhesions, so that at the end of the study only 3.5 percent of the original group remained without a diagnosis. The same author[3] also studied couples who conceived spontaneously early in the course of the infertility investigation prior to receiving any recognized treatment. He found that this group had had relatively low coital exposure (4 times per month for an average of 1.9 years), and that they responded to simple educational talks about the optimal timing and frequency of intercourse for conception. There was no evidence to support the idea that psychophysiologic factors had been significantly altered during the initial clinic visits; this suggested that many of the psychiatric difficulties associated with infertility were secondary to the infertility problem itself and were not primary or causative. They cast serious doubt as to whether psychogenic factors play any role in infertility except in cases of psychogenic impotence and psychogenic failure to ovulate.

I have cited these papers in some detail in order to emphasize a trend away from labeling problems we do not fully understand as psychogenic. A full discussion of the possible causes of male and female infertility is beyond the scope of this discussion, and the reader is referred elsewhere.[4,5] In brief, about 50 percent of all infertility problems are related to factors in the female (the majority of these are problems in tubal patency; the second largest group is related to problems in ovulation). Approximately 30 percent represent problems in the male partner, and are, generally, less amenable to treatment. The remainder represent combined problems for the couple as a unit, with an ever-decreasing percentage representing "unexplained" infertility.

The influence of higher nervous system centers on human reproduction is poorly understood; stress may indeed play a role in ovulation and in spermatogenesis in some individuals, but we have no evidence that the stress is specific. It is overly simplistic to presume, for example, that women with irregular ovulation are in greater conflict about pregnancy, motherhood, or sexuality than are women who ovulate regularly. The old theories of psychogenic infertility have not only been invalidated by recent medical developments, but have generally been counter-productive from both the patients' and therapists' points of view. Patients have avoided contact with psychiatric professionals for fear of being "blamed" or "labeled" pejoratively. Psychotherapy should not and cannot hold out the promise of pregnancy as its goal, although pregnancy may occur during the course of treatment, either spontaneously or as a result of medical or surgical intervention. The legitimate goals of psychotherapy are, in my view, two-fold:

(1) to help the individual or couple deal with the immediate crisis when they recognize that a problem exists and embark on the long, expensive, and often frustrating infertility investigation, and

(2) to help them deal with the longer-term issues of what infertility means to them in the context of their own unique life-experience. The first goal may be achieved in the context of short-term therapy or groups; the second may require more intensive, long-term therapy.

ISSUES IN PSYCHOTHERAPY

Most of the discussion that follows is based on my clinical work,[6,7,8] from 1975 to 1979, with slightly over 100 couples and a few single women, concerned about their infertility. Some were seen for only a few visits in consultation, others for long-term individual or couple therapy. Several had originally sought therapy for generalized depression, but it soon emerged that the infertility issue had been a major precipitant. Most of the patients were seen in private practice, and a few in consultation to the Beth Israel Hospital Infertility Clinic (Boston). In general, the sample was skewed toward middle-class business and professional people between the ages of 28 and 40 who were involved in rather long-term, stable relationships.

Initially, most patients were surprised, even shocked, to learn that they were unable to conceive once the decision to have a baby was made. The decision was often arrived at after years of careful use of birth-control, years of study, training, or career building. Most were distressed and indignant about the loss of control of their life plans implicit in the situation, and many of them handled their feelings of helplessness by becoming experts in areas of particular concern to them. On the whole, these patients were better informed than the average medical school graduate about the physiology of reproduction, significance of various tests (e.g., gonadotropin levels), side effects of treatment modalities, and so on. By and large, this style of defending against helplessness proved to be useful to the patients and allowed them to work collaboratively with the infertility specialist who was treating them. Although an occasional doctor felt threatened by what he or she felt was a questioning of his/her competence and expertise, and an occasional patient was more interested in competitive argument with the doctor than in acquiring information and understanding the process of the infertility investigation.

Most patients seem to go through three phases in dealing with the infertility crisis;[7] these stages may vary in length and often overlap. The first phase revolves around the narcissistic injury. Acknowledgment of an infertility problem, whether it is after six months, one year, or several years of attempting to achieve a pregnancy, is a tremendous blow. Patients are preoccupied with the medical workup and with their own bodies. Prior to this time, many of them have had minimal contact with doctors and have considered themselves as basically healthy people. The infertility study is often a long-term project requiring a high degree of patient participation and cooperation. Other aspects of their lives, such as career plans and social relationships, are often subordinated to the critically timed tests and procedures. Patients must expose their bodies for examination and manipulation; they must reveal intimate details of their sexual lives, and often their private wishes and fears surrounding their desire for a child.

Infertility patients often feel damaged, defective, and "bad." This sense of "badness" may not remain confined to reproductive function alone but may encompass sexual function and desirability, physical attractiveness, performance, and productivity in other spheres as well. Something as basic as core gender identity may be consciously called into question. Several female patients have described feeling like "neuters," not belonging to any group classifiable as male or female; male patients referred to intercourse as "shooting blanks."[5] Concerns about sexual identity and sexual function are almost universal among infertility patients, no matter which partner has the medical problem. In both men and women there is usually a significant diminution of sexual desire, with ejaculatory disturbances of a temporary nature reported by over half of the men.[8,9,10] The depression of both partners consequent to their unsuccessful efforts to achieve a pregnancy, the necessity for sexual relations on demand at specified times in the woman's cycle, and the concern about whether this time will be successful contribute heavily to the problems in sexual function commonly seen in infertile couples.[5,8,9,10] Sex is no longer a spontaneous, pleasurable activity; it is an assignment, a mission with a definable goal, i.e., pregnancy. Although some authors[10] report an increased incidence of promiscuity and extramarital affairs in an effort to "prove" one's masculinity or femininity, in my experience infertile couples complain largely of loss of libido and depression. Many try to be extra good to atone for whatever sins, real or imagined, they may feel caused their infertility.[9] They may carry a heavy load of guilt, sometimes focused on a past event (e.g., an abortion), which may or may not be related to the current problem. Often the guilt is experienced in a diffuse way—guilt about Oedipal wishes, guilt about masturbation, guilt about sexual fantasies of any kind.

There is usually a tremendous escalation of anxiety as the couple awaits the onset of the next menstrual period. The woman becomes preoccupied with changes in her body, searching for signs of pregnancy. All of the tension cannot be attributed to the physiologic changes toward the end of the cycle as many husbands also report great anxiety at this time. Some drugs used to stimulate ovulation, e.g., Clomid, may prolong the second half of the cycle and increase the hope of pregnancy. As the menses begin, many women are plunged into a state of despair—"the cataclysm," as one patient called it; the recurrent barren cycles become exhausting.

Relations between the partners become strained and tense. The infertile spouse may fear actual or emotional abandonment by the other; some will continually test and provoke the partner with comments like, "If you had married someone else you'd have a family by now." The fertile partner may feel an obligation to maintain a front of unswerving loyalty, to disavow any disappointment or anger. In situations where a combined problem exists there may be a great deal of tension around the issue of who is "really to blame" for the problem. And, since the bulk of the tests and diagnostic procedures involve the woman, there may be resentment on her part at having to shoulder most of the responsibility for the workup. The daily basal body temperature charting may serve as a constant reminder that *her* body is not producing a baby, regardless of where the medical problems lie. Some husbands choose to become involved in the temperature charting as a means of affirming their support and involvement.

Oedipal wishes and fears are rekindled with a new intensity—e.g., the wish to present the parent of the opposite sex with the treasured gift of a baby. Some patients have elaborate fantasies about how their infertility is in some way the product of parental revenge; they feel betrayed and "cheated" by the parents who promised them the power to make babies when they grew up.

Rivalry with siblings is reactivated, especially when the siblings have proven their fertility. The jealousy often extends to the entire fertile population. Many patients seriously restrict their lives and cut off old friendships in order to avoid confrontation with pregnant women or families with young babies. The isolation only serves to increase their sense of defectiveness. A peculiar kind of jealousy may emerge in groups of infertile patients. Women who have had a series of miscarriages are viewed as "more fortunate" by those who have never conceived; those who ovulate regularly are seen as "more normal" by those who do not; patients argue about whether it is "better" or "worse" to have a male infertility problem (which is usually less treatable, although the option of donor insemination exists), whether it is "better" or "worse" to have a diagnosis of absolute infertility or to go on thinking that there is a lingering chance for a pregnancy. Themes of deprivation and relative degrees of suffering are common in such groups; rarely will they tolerate a member with a secondary infertility problem (one who has borne a living child), and they have difficulty in dealing with the issue of what to do about group members who become pregnant, with the initial impulse being to expel the offending member.

For many women the wish for the pregnant state, as distinct from parenthood, is endowed with many magical properties. Pregnancy is viewed romantically as the "blossoming" of a woman; labor and delivery are her chances for a starring role.

Many patients see their infertility as a pronouncement of "unfitness" for parenthood. They are disproportionately enraged by those who seem to take it for granted—e.g., people who abuse or neglect their children or those who favor abortion on demand. Some patients express more abstract fears about not being able to produce anything of value, accomplish anything of worth. During the tumult of the infertility workup it is, in fact, more difficult to concentrate on studies or career.

Therapy with patients going through this first phase involves recognizing and acknowledging the feelings evoked by the situation, offering support to help the narcissistic wounds heal, restoring a sense of self-esteem, and helping the patient regain some sense of control over his or her life by clarifying those areas in which elements of choice remain (e.g., choice of a doctor, the timetable for diagnostic and treatment procedures, etc.). It may be sufficient to help patients remember how they have coped with disappointments and frustrations in the past and to remind them to utilize those coping skills in their current situation.

Patients usually enter the second phase when they are ready to call a halt to the infertility investigation. It may be an agonizingly difficult decision, especially for those couples whose infertility remains unexplained or for those who have a small, lingering chance to achieve a pregnancy. During this phase the couple reexamines their own feelings about parenthood and goes through a period of grieving for the loss of their reproductive function, of mourning for the biological children they could not have together. It is in some ways a more painful but less intense process. Although there are now fewer social pressures to have children, for most people parenthood remains an integral part of their development as adults. Frustration in attaining that goal requires a significant reorganization of one's identity in relation to the self and to others.

In her paper *Women and Mid-Life*,[11] Notman discusses how the phases of a woman's life, viewed by herself and others, are often defined by events related to her reproductive function. The awareness of her own mortality, her sense of differentiation from older and younger generations, her assessment of herself in relation to her social environment, are all closely interwoven with the experiences of childbirth, parenting, and the eventual launching of her children into the adult world. Even unmarried or voluntarily childless women may go through a period of depression and mourning somewhere in their thirties or forties, grieving for a part of themselves and for potential life plans that may never be realized.

Most of the literature on male development takes the reproductive role of the male for granted, secondary to the all-important area of work and career development.[12] However, some recent work has examined more thoroughly the meaning of fatherhood to men. Ross's[13] work on *Paternal Identity* is an excellent example. Much of his discussion is applicable to women as well as men, and can also serve as a useful framework in which to examine the difficulties facing the infertile person. In his discussion he defines identity as the individual's continuing sense of self, a very private experience of the self in relation to others.

There are several aspects of identity that are interrelated. During the first year of life the child forms a constant sense of self as distinct from others; in the second year he or she consolidates what Stoller[14] calls "core gender identity," i.e., a firm cognitive and emotional conviction that one is a male or a female and that other people can be similarly classified. Later on a sense of sexual identity emerges, evolving throughout the life cycle, and referring to the sense of the kind of man or woman a person is.

Generational identity refers to the individual's appreciation of where he or she belongs in the generational flow—his or her status as child, parent, grandchild, grandparent.

Parental identity refers to one's fantasies and actual achievements in the imagined or real role of a generator and nurturer of products, human and otherwise. In other words, biological parenthood does not automatically bestow a sense of parental identity, nor is it impossible to achieve a parental identity in the absence of biological parenthood. In some ways the entire developmental process, from infancy onward, is a preparation for forthcoming parenthood, or at least for the capacity to assume a parental role. The decision to have children optimally represents a wish to experience love in a new way, to consolidate a positive identification with parents or parental figures who taught us what love is or should be. There may be self-centered aspects to the desire for children—e.g., fantasies of being reborn, of creating an extension or better version of oneself, of filling a lonely void. For women the wish for the pregnant state may be charged with narcissistic fantasies, with wishes to be valued and admired. To some extent everyone is also ambivalent about becoming a parent. The responsibility is awesome, requiring a major reorganization of one's life style and priorities, sacrifices of freedom and privacy. These fantasies and fears are universal, but the fertile population is afforded the opportunity to test them in reality. The infertile person must struggle harder with them.

Ross[13] discusses how the birth of a first child allows a man to look at his own father in a new light—as a man very much like himself. Until then he may have idealized him or devalued him, but in any case perceived him mainly in relation to this paternal function. Similarly the woman begins to view her mother as a woman like herself with strengths and vulnerabilities. Becoming a parent allows the adult to view the world from the other side of the Us-Them split (with "Us" being the children until that point, "Them" being the parents). The infertile man or woman must work out his or her own ways of renegotiating the relationship with the actual parents of adult life and must put to rest the larger-than-life parents of childhood.

Concerns about generational identity are often expressed in a variety of ways. Many patients express their concern about forever remaining the child of their parents, never fully achieving adult status. Some talk about feeling "old," about being confronted prematurely with a sense of their own mortality (it must be borne in mind that the major non-reproducing populations are the very young and the very old). They worry about being the end of the genetic line. Some patients in my practice who are themselves the children of Holocaust survivors feel this very acutely, as if they must somehow reproduce not only for themselves but for the sake of extended families annihilated during World War II. Others describe their fears of a lonely, grandchildless old age.

Therapy during this phase must focus on the sorting out of issues so that the infertility problem can be put into some perspective in the totality of the patient's life. The individual must reassess his or her own inner resources and make some decision about how best to realize his or her own creative, generative, and nurturant potentials in the absence of biological children. For each individual the resolution of the problem is a very personal matter. At this time, too, the couple must reassess their relationship with each other. Together they must come to terms with the loss of their reproductive function and mourn the loss of the biologic children they could not have together. The infertility experience has the potential to damage or disrupt the relationship; hostility may be generated if one spouse is more heavily invested than the other in having children. There are few social supports to assist the couple in the grieving process because the loss is so vague, invisible, and potential; in a sense they become more dependent on each other for a while. Some couples report that the experience actually brought them closer together, confirming the strength of the bond of love that held them together. In some ways they must complete at an earlier stage a task many couples postpone until after their children are grown.

The third phase involves making some decision about whether and how to pursue the difficult alternate routes to parenthood—adoption, or, in cases of male infertility, artificial insemination by donor. Through this phase the therapist should be aware that there will be a great deal of reworking of old issues. The processes a couple must undergo in order to adopt or use donor insemination are full of their own stresses, discussion of which is beyond the scope of this chapter (see Section II). The loss of the unborn biologic children is periodically remourned, as the world is full of reminders that other people go on having babies. The grief work is never "totally finished," and it is not at all uncommon for the old feelings about infertility to recur at other major transition points in people's lives—retirement, menopause, developments in the lives of adopted children, relatives, and close friends, but it is hoped that the infertile man or woman will have achieved enough satisfaction from life to be able to handle the old disappointment.

The third phase is somewhat different for those couples who do achieve a pregnancy. For them it feels like a "miracle," and they may find that the reality of pregnancy and parenting fails to live up to their long cherished illusions. Or they may feel that they have no right to ambivalent feelings, no right to complain or feel tired; they must be perfect parents and produce a perfect child in order to compensate for their feelings of inadequacy in the area of reproduction. I have been surprised at the number of patients who return to therapy after the birth of a child with concerns about what "normal" parents are supposed to feel. Interestingly, the incidence of clinical depression or other major psychiatric symptoms in the postpartum period seem to be lower among formerly infertile women than in the general population.[5]

For some couples, the third phase may involve the working out of a life style without children that is acceptable to both partners. This may be especially difficult for those couples who have for many years focussed their lives around the single-minded goal of pregnancy. For them the infertility workup and treatment have become a substitute for a child, perhaps their only common interest or the only way in which they can demand or give each other emotional support. It may be difficult to wean such couples from their dependence on their infertility problem (one couple had been working at it for over thirteen years and had seen over ten infertility specialists; they entered psychotherapy seeking a referral for a "new infertility doctor.")

For each individual and couple, the resolution of the problem is unique and is often contingent on prior experiences in coping with disappointment and loss. Patients must prepare themselves to use resources other than reproduction in order to consolidate a comfortable identity as a middle-aged and older adult whether or not parenthood is achieved.

REFERENCES

1. Denber, H.C. Psychiatric aspects of infertility. *Journal of Reproductive Medicine 20* (1), 23–9, Jan. 1978.

2. Drake, T., & Tredway, D. Spontaneous pregnancy during the infertility evaluation. *Fertility and Sterility 29* (1), 36–38, July 1978.

3. Drake, T., Buchanan, G., Takaki, N., & Deane, T.A. Unexplained infertility: a reappraisal. *Obstetrics and Gynecology 50* (644), 1977.

4. Taymor, M.L. *Infertility.* New York: Grune and Stratton, 1978.

5. Menning, B.E. *Infertility: a guide for the childless couple.* Englewood Cliffs, New Jersey: Prentice-Hall, 1977.

6. Mazor, M. The problem of infertility. *The woman patient,* Vol. I, Ch. 11, pp. 137–160, eds. M. Notman and C. Nadelson, New York: Plenum, 1978.

7. Mazor, M. Barren couples. *Psychology Today* (May 1979).

8. Mazor, M. Psychosexual problems of the infertile couple. *Medical Aspects of Human Sexuality,* Vol. 14, No. 12, Dec. 1980.

9. Debrovner, C., & Shubin-Stein, R. Sexual problems associated with infertility, *Medical Aspects of Human Sexuality,* Mar. 1976, pp. 161–162.

10. Walker, H.E. Sexual problems and infertility. *Psychosomatics 19* (8), 477–484, Aug. 1978.

11. Notman, M. Women and mid-life: a different perspective. *Psychiatric Opinion 15* (9), 15, Sept. 1978.

12. Levinson, D., Darrow, C., et al. *The seasons of a man's life.* New York: Knopf, 1978.

13. Ross, J.M. Paternal identity: reflections on the adult crisis and its developmental reverberations. *On sexuality: psychoanalytic observations,* eds. T. Byram Karasu and C.W. Socarides, New York: International Univ. Press, 1979.

14. Stoller, R. *Sex and Gender.* New York: Science House, 1968.

Chapter 4

A HOLISTIC APPROACH TO THE TREATMENT OF INFERTILITY

Ellen K. Bresnick*

It will be the purpose of this paper to discuss some of the psychological implications of infertility and the need to understand its particular place in the milieu of psychological treatment. Most of the information presented is based on referrals from a private medical group that specializes in the treatment of infertility. A psychotherapeutic referral is available to everyone who comes to this office regardless of overt need. These referrals should be made in conjunction with a total medical work-up. Patients are seen either in the doctor's office or in a private office. They are given the options of joining a short term group, being seen privately with spouse, or being seen individually. Any one or none of the combinations could be accepted by the patient. From March 1975 to January 1978 approximately 80 couples accepted a referral.

It is currently recognized that the problem of infertility

---

*Reprinted from Volume 7, Number 2 of the *Journal of Marital and Family Therapy*, Copyright 1981, American Association for Marriage and Family Therapy. Reprinted by permission.

has two components: a medical component and a psychological component. Medically, infertility is defined as an inability to conceive successfully after one year of actively attempting conception. Psychologically, infertility creates a condition conceptualized as the "crisis of infertility." This state is an emotional condition that gives rise to feelings of loss—loss of health, loss of self-esteem, and feelings of mourning, depression, guilt, and frustration. It creates social conditions of isolation and career and job problems and places many stresses in a marriage, particularly in the spheres of communication, sexual activity, and future planning. Whatever one's emotional state prior to infertility, the presence of the crisis itself has the potential to exacerbate or reactivate any emotional conflicts. The presence of emotional stress may have an effect on the biological functioning of an individual, particularly on the endocrine and hormone balance; thus the "crisis of infertility" itself can set into motion a cycle that has the potential to perpetuate itself.

It becomes the job of mental health workers to intervene in the emotional aspects of infertility and alleviate the stresses aroused by the condition. The timing of this intervention and the role of the therapist continues to need investigation, but the need can no longer be overlooked.

Three psychological-behavioral categories have been conceptualized:

1. The first category consists of those individuals or couples who, prior to the crisis of infertility, suffered from severe psychopathology, and consequent behavioral dysfunction. The onset of the crisis of infertility is an extension of the existing psychopathology and its accompanying behavioral dysfunction.

2. The second category consists of individuals or couples who superficially function fairly well prior to the onset of the infertility crisis despite the existence of underlying pathology with potential to erupt into behavioral disturbances. In this category the psychological stress of infertility is so

pressing that the pathology is activated and the individuals involved seem to function less successfully.

3. The third category consists of those couples who could be considered "normal," people who have demonstrated adaptive coping mechanisms in other situations. In this group of cases, the onset of the crisis of infertility causes tremendous emotional distress and accompanying behavioral problems. Once the situation is alleviated or resolved, these people are able to resume their "normal" functioning.

In the first category there is a history of severe pathology. In many of these cases, the couple merely use their infertility as a vehicle for referral, yet quickly reveal a more extensive pathological situation—i.e., a history of inadequate emotional and social relations prior to the recognition of infertility. Often only one spouse accepts referral (a situation by itself not indicative of pathology). Some cling to the infertility as the only source of their problems. They deny the value of therapy feeling the only cure to their problems would be a pregnancy. On the other hand, they may utilize the infertility as a reason for accepting psychological help. Some are willing to use the opportunity for therapy to work on some of their more disruptive pathology. Some can benefit from work on just the infertility itself.

A case in this first category is presented below:

Case 1:

Mr. and Mrs. C. have been married for five years, four of which have been concerned with achieving pregnancy. Mrs. C. is four years older than Mr. C. and is of a foreign, racially mixed background. She is a college graduate and had been employed in a helping profession for the last ten years. Mr. C., a high school graduate, is of Jewish background and is a steadily employed blue collar worker. Mr. and Mrs. C. were being seen together at an outpatient clinic because of her severe depression. Because her infertility problem became a more central issue in therapy, she was referred to me. Both she and her husband accepted the referral. They have been seen together on a weekly basis for over a year.

Mrs. C. presents herself as a very quiet, neat, sad lady who seldom smiles and is reluctant to show any affect other than frequent tears. She is readily compliant with many of her husband's rules and requests but often responds to him with a flat, affectless concurrence. Mr. C. is often teasing and superficial, and readily hides behind his "ignorance" and lack of education when any emotional insights or feelings are evoked. He tends to "explain" and interpret behaviors and feelings on a simplistic and, at times, concrete level of understanding. When feelings of too much dissension are raised, Mr. C. wonders if that's not life and "what can you do?" Mr. C. seldom became upset or concerned with Mrs. C.'s frequent crying, sleepless nights and, at times, overwhelming fears of impending danger. His response is generally "that's the way she is." There is seldom concern for the impact of their own behaviors on one another.

Mr. C. described himself as a juvenile delinquent with a lack of enthusiasm for achievement. He was one of four children raised in a lower-class ghetto. His father was seldom home, having to work two jobs. His mother was completely involved at home, frantically attempting to achieve order and cleanliness at home with her children. Mr. C. seldom attended high school, was often truant and frequently participated in mildly disruptive social behavior.

Mrs. C. came from an upwardly mobile home in a foreign country. She is the middle of three sisters approximately two and a half years apart. Her parents were interracially and inter-culturally married with two of the three girls having oriental appearances. They operated a successful small general store. The family lived in back of the store. The girls either spent after school hours in the store or frequently had sitters to care for them. The father was described as volatile, combative, and seldom warm and loving in his behavior. The mother was described as very nervous and reportedly suffered severe breakdowns resulting in weeks in bed and numerous threats of suicide. Mrs. C. recalls constantly fearing impending danger and remembers sitting by her mother's bed for days so that she would be there if needed. She recalls feeling extreme homesickness when sent to boarding school. She was subsequently moved to a second school closer to home. Upon coming to the U.S. to complete her education, she reported several occasions where she "couldn't cope with the pressures." She remembers crying uncontrollably and wanting to kill herself.

Both Mr. and Mrs. C. felt totally befuddled by their infertility. Mrs. C. felt this was what she deserved but expressed great ambivalence regarding the responsibilities of parenthood. She cried readily, fearing her parents would not live long enough to see a grandchild. She felt competitive and jealous that her younger and also infertile sister would conceive before herself. She expressed fear that Mr. C. had no reason to stay in the marriage if she couldn't conceive. There was no known medical reason for their failure to conceive except possibly an inadequate luteal phase.

Mr. C. just wanted a child; being a father would be proof of his manliness, but he felt confused by his parents' warning that racially mixed children were genetically unsound.

Initially, both concurred that Mrs. C.'s depression would magically disappear if only pregnancy would occur.

In the first part of our treatment, we spent a great deal of time educating and focusing on the medical aspects of the infertility. Through the discussions of the social and medical aspects of infertility we had an opportunity to view the passive, helpless, victimized positions they readily found themselves in as couples and individually. They were both gradually able to move from their rigid positions to comprehension of Mrs. C.'s depression and were able to view this as a chronic symptom that needed attention with or without a pregnancy. They accepted the challenge to view their problems in a more pervasive, introspective manner, having built trust and confidence with the therapist through the infertility work.

Mr. & Mrs. C. eventually conceived. The pregnancy was filled with turmoil because of the confusing results of an amniocentesis. The delays and retesting resulted in the resurgence of Mrs. C.'s severe depression, anxiety, and fear. She wept almost constantly, walked the floors at night, and openly struggled with her fantasies of a "monstrous" child. My work focused on the realities of that testing process as well as her behavior and feelings. By the time of her delivery, they both experienced enough support, education, and insight to be able to allow themselves the mutual thrill of the joy of childbirth. A potential postpartum depression seemed averted as they were more in touch with their true feelings utilizing the insights and support gained during our long-term therapeutic relationship.

There is no intention to imply in any way the role of their psychological state on their infertility, but rather the impact of the infertility on their general life style. In this case therapy was offered in view of the infertile status and, as a result, many gains as well as preventions have been achieved for this couple whose already fragile existence was more severely handicapped by the occurrence of the infertility.

In this case much work was done around the infertility crisis itself. Work often focused a great deal on the testing being done, interpreting temperature charts and the effect of the work-up, as well as on the subsequent disappointment in themselves, their marriage, and their relationships outside their home. The encouragement to express and look at the problems aroused by the infertility itself provided a supportive opportunity to share many of the angers, disappointments, and feelings of failure that they had kept to themselves. The education surrounding the medical aspects of infertility helped both feel more confident and responsible as well as involved in their subsequent treatment. The couple expressed increased feelings of confidence and importance as they related to their doctors. The presence of the infertility did, however, continue to feed the individuals' already low self-esteem and provided excuses for marital disappointments. It perpetuated the daily struggle for personal contact, self-worth, and communication that already interfered with their general abilities to cope and plan for the future.

Regardless of the underlying pathology, the treatment of the infertility itself prevented the psychological side effects from expanding; it allowed both partners a chance to attempt mature communication in sharing an issue that was common to both.

Nonetheless, therapeutic intervention for the crisis of infertility helped prevent further personal deterioration that seemed to be snowballing at the time of the initial referral.

As mentioned earlier, the second category of couples consisted of persons who managed to make adequate life adjustments despite underlying potential pathology; marriage and general life styles were reportedly satisfactory, yet infertility seemed to promote a situation that constantly tested the individuals' ego strengths and defenses used to protect the onslaught of negative feelings aroused by the constant failure to successfully reproduce. When individuals want something badly enough to work hard for it, constant failure cannot go unnoticed. The more difficult a pregnancy seems to be to achieve, the harder a couple must work if they have any intention of succeeding. Every month menstruation occurs there is a sense of failure. Many people function well in their marriages and jobs providing no external crises arise. The fact of infertility is such an external crisis. An example of this situation is as follows:

Case 2:

Mr. and Mrs. V. are a couple in their middle thirties and have been married for six years, actively trying conception for four. Mrs. V. did conceive in the beginning of their efforts but had an uncomplicated miscarriage in the first trimester. They were making one last effort to have a child when they were referred to me as part of the routine work-up.

The V.'s initially presented an uneventful history and superficially seemed to accept their infertility—i.e., if we have a child, great—if not, we would accept that, too. None of us felt further contact was indicated, but the V.'s did feel they wanted to attend a three-week group session that the doctor and I periodically offered new patients in the office. It was following these sessions that Mrs. V. asked to see me alone.

Mrs. V. then revealed an early history of some disrupture. Prior to her marriage she had had an abortion, then the miscarriage, and she was now unable to conceive. She felt perhaps she must be doing something to punish herself. She had considered adoption, but her husband's earlier history perhaps precluded that option. The V.'s subsequently came together for several months.

They used therapy to renegotiate their disruptive past and to reexperience the heartache of Mr. V.'s previous marriage and the handicapped child resulting from that marriage. Dissolution of his first marriage had been extremely volatile and destructive and had ended with Mr. V. surrendering the child for adoption to his alcoholic ex-wife. Reliving of the past gave Mr. V. a chance to grieve over his loss and to look at the options for the future. They slowly began to uncover their own histories and the overwhelming feelings that the other would reject himself/herself for their separate "sins" of the past. What actually was revealed was a great deal of caring for one another and a strong desire for both to become parents together. The risks of sharing this were great, for once they knew how much they wanted a child they would then have to face the possibility that they couldn't have one. We then had the opportunity to deal with the option of adoption and their fears of rejection because of their past history.

Furthermore, during the course of our work together they revealed sexual problems. With much talking and sharing the impact of the infertility on their sex life, they were able to use the knowledge and help to have relations at the optimal time during the course of their treatment. They both expressed a great deal of relief from discussing their sexual activity with an authoritative figure in whom they felt great trust and confidence.

The V.'s therapy included a great deal of education in current medical status as well as dealing with problems rearoused because of the infertility. The V.'s had felt their past history would interfere with their chances of adoption and thus, in order to protect themselves from the potential failure of not having a family, they denied their own true needs and wants. They closed off many avenues of feelings and sharings between them to support their mutual need to deny wanting a child. Therapy allowed them to face their true feelings and ultimately helped them chance the pursuance of adoption. The increased ability to share and their increased education of the impact of infertility on all aspects of their life allowed for successful intervention with their deteriorated, problematic sex life. Without this opportunity the V.'s would undoubtedly have committed themselves to an unwanted, unaccepted life as a childless couple never taking the full chances to either reproduce successfully themselves or to adopt. In the face of the infertility crisis, their past history had been tucked away only to be recalled and to resurface in a negative way with their current lives.

Let it be noted that during the entire course of long-term treatment Mrs. V. eventually conceived only to have a tragic miscarriage at five months of pregnancy. Nonetheless, they were able to continue to buy a home for themselves and are now the proud parents of an adopted infant. They periodically continue contact with me as they embark on their new life as parents. This seemingly casual routine referral provided an opportunity to look at the overall impact of infertility on a couple whose level of functioning had become seriously impaired as a past history clearly increased and exacerbated the negative impact of infertility on this couple.

In this case the crisis of infertility exacerbated and aroused what was considered by them as "resolved" pathology. In therapy Mr. V. managed to make many breaks from his past and was able appropriately to mourn the "loss" of his child by his previous marriage. He was able to share this with his wife who was also able to offer support, understanding, and strength. Had infertility not occurred, this couple probably would have managed a family with little difficulty. The availability of counseling through the infertility issue opened the door for continued growth. With appropriate therapeutic intervention around a specific crisis, the Achilles' heel can become a strength. This functioning couple might have gone through their lives denying their pain and closing off avenues of communication by which they had felt so overwhelmed and for which they were so ill equipped to face.

The issue of infertility again provided an appropriate opportunity to deal safely with potentially disruptive pathology in a highly motivated couple.

The third category of infertility patients is the "normal"

couple. This group is composed of individuals who are functioning on many levels consistent with their own expectations and
general life. They have good relationships with family, friends,
and community. However, gradually they have found themselves tormented by frequent feelings of depression, anger, isolation, and jealousy. They feel confused and threatened in their
marital relationship. Their sexual life seems to have many problems and they find themselves filled with feelings of jealousy
and resentment, particularly toward their pregnant friends and
relatives. They are unable to share their friends' joys around
children and/or pregnancy. They begin to feel different. They,
at times, diagnostically can present an acute state of mourning.
It seems overwhelming and endless, yet they strongly feel that if
they could only have a baby everything would be all right.

For this group this is by and large a seeming truth and reality. This is the first time the partners have faced a problem in
their marriage or life for which they don't have the tools or
models with which to cope. They suddenly find themselves in
the doctor's office at least once a month. They watch their temperature charts and carefully guide their sex life to make sure
they hit the exact moment. They invest their energies, hopes,
and dreams into something they know they might never achieve.
Yet without the efforts, the doctor's visits, the obedience to tests,
they are reasonably sure they will also fail to achieve a successful
pregnancy. They are in the hands of fate, luck, and some good
medical care. If things were different, if they became pregnant
easily, they would not be involved with the "crisis of infertility."
They would not be coping with the daily pressures of failure,
feelings of anger, frustration, and jealousy and would not be
forced to seriously evaluate their expectations or reasons for
wanting a family. They now might have to place themselves at
the mercy of an adoption worker who will decide whether or not
they were "acceptable" parents or they may have to consider going through life together without any children after they have
made the choice to have children.

These are extremely stressful life decisions that have to be
faced in the event that pregnancy is unlikely or impossible.
These are only some of the questions they must deal with and

only after they have faced what it means to them not to bear a genetic child, not to reproduce, particularly when they have already made a choice to do so.

The following is an example of a category 3 couple. After five years of marriage and active attempts to achieve pregnancy, they referred themselves to a private office that specialized in the diagnosis and treatment of infertility.

Case 3:

Mr. and Mrs. L. are a couple in their early thirties who have been trying to reproduce for all of their five years of marriage. They decided to legalize their relationship so they could have the family they both wanted.

Mr. and Mrs. L. presented a picture of two well-defended persons who had clearly been struggling with the anger, frustration, and hurt that accompany the infertility syndrome. They were both volatile, and their struggle has taken its toll in numerous arguments as each felt unworthy of the other and each was overwhelmed by the constant failure. Nonetheless, they used humor appropriately with and about themselves and each other. They sought good medical treatment, were responsible throughout, and had clearly made great efforts to understand the purposes of the test results and treatment. They had developed a strong communication between themselves and seemed to show a genuine warm love and affection for one another. They both felt the infertility had made it more difficult for them to develop strong social ties as it was often painful to be with pregnant women or little children. They applied for adoption but they felt it wouldn't be necessary and that it really wasn't for them. They were somewhat reluctant to become directly involved with me, feeling they were in full control of a situation in which they were helpless victims.

Medical results revealed a history of unexplained poor post-coital tests and occasional low sperm counts, occasional poor ovulation, and severe endometriosis. Despite their denial and appropriate confusion regarding medical problems, they were responsible and thorough in their pursuit and follow up of all medical options. Mrs. L. underwent a laparotomy for her increasingly severe endometriosis. She awoke to learn that an ovary and a tube had been removed. She relied heavily on denial to deal with the severity of her condition.

Mr. L. is the second of two siblings; he has an older sister. His sister also had a history of infertility, but finally had been able to conceive and have two children. His mother also had a history of infertility. Mr. L. lost a twin brother at birth. Despite the unavailability of a thorough history of Mr. L.'s youth, it was by and large described as uneventful. Mr. L. currently works with his father in a family business. No outstanding problems were related. Mr. L. feels his parents are reasonably close to him but clearly resents their lack of "compassion" and understanding regarding their childlessness. He feels envious and deprived as he relates his parents' joy with his sister's child and new pregnancy. Mr. L. revealed a fantasy that his parents would possibly become more involved with them if they had children. He did not feel they were as warm and understanding as he would have liked them to be or as he hopes to be as a parent.

Mrs. L. is also the youngest of three, with a sister twelve years her senior and a brother six years older. Both are married with children. Her mother also had a history of infertility and seems to vacillate between understanding and support and frustration and guilt concerning her daughter's plight. Mrs. L.'s father died suddenly during the winter prior to her meeting Mr. L. She revealed a close and supportive relationship with her father and she talked of his loss with great pain. Mrs. L. spoke of her mother as having a history of numerous medical problems that seemed to stir anxiety and confusion as Mrs. L.'s health seemed questionable in relation to the infertility. She reviews her childhood as one filled with many struggles to achieve happiness and success. She sees her infertility as a continuation of having to struggle for what she wants.

Mrs. L. was seen alone in therapy several times and then conjointly with Mr. L. They also opted to participate in a three-week group program. Following the initial contact, they periodically kept in touch with me to share important events.

As this couple is placed in category 3, it is important to note how the "crisis of infertility" exacerbates and/or activates old psychological and emotional events. Note how the loss of Mr. L.'s twin brother rears it subtle impact as he hopes to please his parents with a "son". The pain of Mrs. L.'s brother's twins is greater as they acknowledge that this is what they have wanted so badly. Mrs. L. had readily remourned her father's death as she spoke of her "loss" of the child. Their constant need to look over their past as they search for some understanding of "why me?" is pressing in their day to day life. Even though they now have an adopted child who has clearly fulfilled so many of their needs and hopes, they are currently again faced with many of the old infertility issues as they try for a second child.

Although the L.'s appeared to be a fairly strong, insightful couple who had worked through and shared many thoughts, feelings, and fantasies about their infertility, they were well able to utilize the support and education offered through infertility counseling. Their attendance, active participation, and intermittent contact over a two-year-period is clearly indicative of their need to talk and be heard. They readily used me as a resource for coping with and understanding medical issues. Of tremendous importance was their use of me to help them prepare for their probable adoption of a child. They shared their fears and anxieties, clearly feeling more confident and comfortable as the probability of adoption became a reality. They were able to use our relationship to help them emotionally prepare and facilitate the impending adoption.

Note that this couple is defined as the "otherwise normal" couple who are victims of the "infertility crisis," in spite of the fact that pathological behavior or feelings might be observed. Classification of normal is derived primarily from the efficient adaptive mechanisms of these individuals.

It is clear that many of the psychological issues of infertility need to be scientifically explored. The role of counseling and the coping with the crisis of infertility continue to need evaluation. The success of therapeutic intervention is not to be considered in terms of achieved pregnancy but, rather, as part of a total outlook of resolution for a particular couple in relation to their own emotional status prior to the onset of the crisis. Because of the numerous variables in the selection and acceptance of case referrals, it is quite probable that the pathology or status of patients is skewed. Nonetheless, it is apparent that infertility tends to arouse, perpetuate, and exacerbate psychological and emotional turmoil that can be successfully treated by therapeutic intervention regardless of the diagnosis and the outcome of the infertility condition.

At the very least the minimum therapeutic goal should be concerned with the impact of concurrent medical and physical events involved in the infertility work-up. Constant education and expanded awareness of available medical tests and of the reasons for them as well as an evaluation of the results and treatment are related to the feelings of helplessness and loss of control experienced by patients. Education about their medical aspects of infertility begins to provide a basis for communication and involvement between the partners if the therapist can continue to help the clients investigate the deep emotional impacts of the "crisis," and can help direct them to a successful grieving of the very real "loss" of a biological ability to perpetuate themselves. The social implications of the "incomplete" marital unit can also be explored.

Helping clients to face the biological, emotional, and social implications created by the status of infertility can be a positive major contribution by mental health professionals in continuing to recognize individuals as total beings. The crisis of infertility involves a holistic approach to mental health. The body and mind are inseparable.

The infertility questionnaire was part of a study by Ellen Bresnick and Dr. Melvin Taymor. The data and results were presented at the Annual Conference of the American Fertility Society in March of 1978. The questionnaire asked individuals to grade on a 1 to 5 basis the presence of their feelings of guilt, anger, frustration, and isolation—5 was the highest degree of symptomatology. Question 2 evaluated the problem areas: communication with spouse, sexual adjustment, career attitudes, and attitude toward possible fertility failure. Of the 111 questionnaires sent to patients whom I saw over a two-year-period,

Infertility Counseling Questionnaire

I. Effect of counseling sessions on symptoms possibly caused by your infertility.

Mark each category on a 1 to 5 basis (5 being the strongest feeling)
Example—*very* angry = 5; a little frustrated = 2.

	Before counseling	*After counseling*
1. Feelings of guilt		
2. Feelings of anger		
3. Feelings of frustration		
4. Feelings of isolation		

II. Problem areas before and after counseling.

(1 being poor; 5 being excellent)
Example—Poor communication with spouse = 1; excellent communication = 5

	Before counseling	*After counseling*
Communication with spouse		
Sexual adjustment		
Attitude toward career or job		
Attitude toward possible failure of fertility		

III. General Questions

1. Sex (Circle One)   Male   Female
2. What type of sessions did you attend? Check all applicable.
   A. Group   _____
   B. Couple alone   _____
   C. Individual   _____
3. How many sessions did you attend? _____
4. When was your last session?   _____
5. What areas in your life were most affected or improved by the sessions? (Indicate 1st, 2nd, 3rd choice in order of importance.)
   a. Communication with spouse   _____
   b. Understanding of medical tests and treatment   _____
   c. Your job plans   _____
   d. Your educational plans   _____
   e. Your moods   _____
   f. Your sexual relationship   _____
   g. Your overall daily outlook   _____
6. Your overall evaluation of the sessions is (check one):
   Very helpful _____ Somewhat helpful _____ Of little help _____

56 questionnaires were returned, just over 50 percent. This high statistic may possibly be indicative of the investment of the participants. All results pointed to a statistically significant amelioration of symptoms indicating emotional turmoil, as well as an apparent diminution of problem areas in daily functioning. Forty-nine respondees stated that they found therapeutic contact, regardless of quantity of visits or diagnosis of infertility, to be at least somewhat helpful.

The need for, and potential value of, psychiatric intervention with couples involved in the crisis of infertility is clearly becoming a professional mandate.

REFERENCES

Benedek, T., Ham, G.C., Robbins, F.P., & Rubenstein, B.B. Some emotional factors in infertility, *Psychosomatic Medicine 15* (485), 1953.

Berger, D.M. Psychological assessment of the infertile couple. *Canadian Family Physician, 20* (89), 1975.

Berger, D.M. The role of the psychiatrist in a reproductive biology clinic. *Fertility & Sterility, 28* (141–5), Feb. 1977.

Bresnick, E.K. Infertility counseling, *Infertility*, M.L. Taymor, ed., Ch. 15, pp. 94–98. New York: Grune & Stratton, 1978.

Denber, H.C. Psychiatric aspects of infertility. *Journal of Reproductive Medicine 20* (1, 23–9), Jan. 1978.

Eisner, B.G. Some psychological differences between fertile and infertile women. *Journal Clinical Psychology 19* (391), 1963.

Mai, F.M., Munday, R.N., & Rump, E.E. Psychiatric interview comparisons between fertile and infertile couples. *Psychosomatic Medicine 4* (431), 1972.

Mazor, M. The problem of infertility, in M. Notman and C. Nadelson, eds. *The woman patient.* Vol. I, Ch. 11, pp. 137–160. New York: Plenum, 1978.

McGuire, L.S. Obstetrics and gynecology: psychologic management of the infertile woman. *Postgraduate Medicine 57* (6); 173–6, May 1975.

Wilchins, S.A. The use of group 'rap sessions' in the adjunctive treatment of five infertile females. *Journal of the Medical Society of New Jersey 71* (12):951–3, Dec. 1974.

Chapter 5

RESOLVE
Counseling and Support for
Infertile Couples

Barbara Eck Menning

Since 1973 I have been involved in the counseling of people with
infertility problems. I arrived at this unusual specialization as a
consequence of my personal experience with infertility and my
professional experience in maternity and pediatric nursing. My
personal experience with infertility encompassed four years of
testing and attempted treatment, which concluded in the realiza-
tion that I would never be able to bear a child. I found this period of my life very stressful and sought therapy to work through
the troublesome issues. After I had settled my own feelings, I
proceeded to adopt a family of three multiracial children. I was
concerned that there might be other people with problems related to infertility and turned my energies toward finding them.

My first counseling experience actually came from an adoptive parents' organization, the Open Door Society. The helpful
volunteers in this organization referred many "new inquiry"
callers to me for information about adoption. Many of these
callers had recently discovered their infertility problem and
were just beginning to think about alternatives. I tended to explore with the callers a little of their infertility background. I was
struck by how many of these people had never really addressed

their grief over the loss of the childbearing experience, or how many had been managed poorly, or not at all, during their infertility workup. After a time I became more and more an infertility counselor and less and less an adoption counselor. There seemed to be many helpful and capable people working in adoption assistance, but at that time few if any professionals were working with the problem of the emotional impact of infertility.

I started an organization called RESOLVE; the name is not an acronym, but is the word which best states what we hope to achieve—resolution of the state of longing to have children and being unable to. The state is not always resolved by pregnancy—in fact, only about half of infertility is "cured" by medical intervention. We try to help people resolve their feelings and get on with their lives; this can mean selection of an alternative way of family building, acceptance of a life without children, or successful pregnancy and childbirth.

Since 1973 RESOLVE has grown from a kitchen table voluntary project to one now national in scope. We are incorporated and nonprofit, with headquarters in Boston and chapters, at the time of this writing, in 43 cities around the country. Our membership is about five thousand couples strong. Our funding comes from membership dues, which bring our bimonthly Newsletter, and from the sale of various literature about infertility and alternatives, as well as from contributions.

We have come a long way since 1973, and the only reason this has happened is because there is a great need—a need for advocacy and support in the infertile population. Although they number in excess of 10 million people, infertile people are entirely invisible in this society and do not know how to contact each other. Therefore, they have never organized and have not known how to pressure for improved services or how to implement changes. Now, through RESOLVE, we at least have a beginning.

An illustration of the saga of many infertile couples is that they become concerned, after varying periods of time, that attempts at pregnancy and childbirth seem to elude them. They may first consult a family doctor or general practitioner for a beginning investigation. If this fails to reveal and cure the problem, they often seek a "second opinion," the woman from a gynecologist, the man from a urologist. Failing success at this level, the couple may seek out the advice of an infertility specialist, or even several consecutive "expert" opinions. All along there may be token or attempted emotional support and education from the doctor and his/her staff—the nurse, the technician, even the receptionist. Sometimes social services of a hospital are called in to work with the distressed couple. Some couples or individuals seek psychotherapy for themselves because they are disturbed about their own feelings. If medical efforts fail the couple may turn to adoption as an alternative. In each of these situations there may be professional staff with areas of expertise that may be helpful, in part, to the infertile couple. But the sum total of all their efforts may still be a patchwork at best, or a tugging of cross-purposes at worst. Who, then, is the advocate of the infertile couple? I think, in all fairness, that we have to agree that they have to be their own advocates to get through the labyrinth of infertility investigation and attempted treatment, and, if not successful, to locate an alternative and get on with their lives.

RESOLVE is an advocacy organization that encourages infertile people to educate themselves so that they can make informed decisions about their own health care. We urge them to seek out the most qualified physicians they can find. We inform them that they have a right to expect physicians and their staffs to be considerate of their feelings, tolerant of questions, and willing to develop an infertility investigation and treatment regimen according to a mutually agreed upon plan and pace. At RESOLVE our stated objectives are these: to offer infertility counseling, referral, and support. Referral may be to a first, second, or even tenth opinion on the infertility problem. People come at all stages of investigation. Referral may also be to a source of help for alternatives, such as adoption or donor insemination. We consider child-free living a viable alternative, too, and represent this very fairly in our literature, counseling, and support groups. Sometimes we make a referral to a source of counseling or therapy beyond our scope. Sexual problems, marital problems, and deep-seated psychological issues are examples of issues we are not equipped to treat at this time. Our final service is support. This is no small task when one considers the often protracted case histories, the societal and familial pressures to bear children, and the emotional stresses brought to bear upon two members of a couple. We offer support groups for couples or women who wish to come together and share experiences with one another.

Telephone counseling is available from our Boston headquarters 9 A.M. to 4 P.M. on weekdays. Trained counselors are available to answer basic questions about reproduction, infertility tests and treatments, and optimal timing and technique for conception. Our counselors respect the limits of their expertise and do not attempt to make diagnoses or recommend a plan of therapy over the phone. Medical advisers are available for more technical questions. We do a lot of reading and research and attempt to stay current. All telephone counseling is kept in strictest confidence and is a free service, available to anyone who wishes to call.

Crisis intervention counseling is another service we offer to individuals or couples, in the office, by appointment. The appropriate client is one who is perplexed and unable to decide about what to do next in the infertility work-up or selection of an alternative. Clients usually request an opportunity to talk with someone in order to focus on what has been done and what options remain open. There is a large educational component in such counseling, and generous support is offered for the painful feelings involved. Frequently one or two visits will help the person or couple define their problem and decide on a course of action. By definition, crisis intervention counseling is short-term (usually six sessions or less), focuses on the immediate past, the present, and near future, and deals with a well-defined issue or set of issues. Clients who need longer term counseling are referred to an appropriate therapist when that need has been established. Our office fee is based on a sliding scale according to ability to pay.

Peer support groups are undoubtedly our most successful means of offering emotional support. It is striking how similar the problems and issues of the groups have been even though the circumstances and personalities of the participants have been extremely varied. Initially we offered groups for women, because that request was most frequently made; lately, because of the greater number of inquiries from men and couples, we are offering more couples' groups and fewer women's groups. Most RESOLVE chapters around the country currently offer at least one support group.

The support groups seem to work best when led by a trained professional leader. Issues of infertility are often intense and painful. The presence of a leader is reassuring to the group members and helps them focus on appropriate areas. Leaders come from a variety of backgrounds including nursing, psychiatric social work, and counseling. They usually have graduate level training and previous experience with group work. The names of people interested in joining the support groups come from a variety of sources including general publicity in the media, doctors, adoption agencies, and word of mouth. In the Boston area we offer one round of support groups in the fall, approximately 15 weekly sessions from September to January, and a second round of support groups from late winter through the middle of June, also for 15 sessions.

The support group leader receives a list of interested people and is responsible for screening the individual or couple for appropriateness for the group. It is important to stress that a support group is *not* a therapy group. The ideal group member is a normally functioning person struggling with a stressful infertility situation that is causing painful feelings and a sense of isolation and depression. We attempt to screen out those people who are massively depressed, those who have a distorted sense of reality, and those for whom the infertility problem is not the central issue but rather a reactivator of other deep-seated issues of loss that have not been worked through. These people are often referred for individual therapy or evaluation for therapy in another setting.

The optimal group size seems to be about eight individuals or four couples, plus the leader. Groups with as many as ten members have been run successfully, but a group is not started unless there are at least five members. Membership is kept open until either enough members have been added or the group members decide that they would like to close the group. Usually enough trust and cohesion has developed by the third or fourth session to make the introduction of new members difficult after that time. Meetings are held weekly, usually at the leader's home in the evening, and last from one and a half to two hours. The members pay a nominal fee, from which the leader receives a salary.

RESOLVE support groups are time-limited and issue oriented. This is a very important aspect of this model. It encourages the participants to get involved, to get to work on feelings and issues, and then to face the reality of termination by discovering personal strengths and social supports that can continue to alleviate the distress of the infertility experience. The role of the leader is to facilitate discussion, to attempt to keep it at a feeling level, to model appropriate behavior, and to reinforce positive insights and growth. Although old issues are occasionally reviewed in groups, there is no attempt to analyze them. Group members get a great deal of support from each other, but they may also get some confrontation and negative feedback. In my experience some of the best growth and change and the closest sharing may take place after such confrontations. An area in which I feel that I have matured as a group leader is that of being more comfortable with negative remarks and less likely to rush to a person's defense.

There is a definite educational component to support groups as well. Participants learn to be their own advocates and to negotiate better for what they need and want from the health care systems or from other institutions such as adoption agencies. A support group offers a unique and confidential milieu for sharing and validating feelings; it is a safe place to be angry or to begin one's grieving. Many support group members continue contact and friendship long after the formal group has terminated.

I would like to share a few comparisons between the community-based groups we offer at RESOLVE and agency-based groups that some doctors and institutions offer. I accept the right and need for all to exist; certainly all are geared toward helping the infertile couple. I prefer the RESOLVE model for a number of reasons. First, because we are divided along geographical lines instead of by a particular clientele, we serve people with a variety of problems and in all stages of resolution. We also serve the clients of a variety of physicians and this allows for greater sharing of experience. All people who enter our support groups are self-referred. Occasionally we have had problems with adoption agencies who have made a strong suggestion to a couple that they are not "resolved" about their infertility feelings and that they ought to enroll in one of our groups before entering or continuing a home study. RESOLVE is very reluctant to accept anyone on such a basis. We think that self-referral indicates a point of *readiness* important for success. Furthermore, we can in no way ensure that a person or couple will leave the support group "resolved" in their feelings.

RESOLVE support groups are confidential; our leaders are not employed by health care providers or adoption agencies with which the members are working directly. Many of the leaders have themselves experienced infertility and are in a good position to understand and empathize with the members' situations.

In contrast, the agency sponsored or clinic sponsored support groups, althogh described as purely "voluntary", may be subtly coercive if the client perceives that he or she will receive more attention or better care if group meetings are attended. This has been a particularly important issue in pre- and post-adoptive groups, where there is a very significant payoff. If a couple is hoping to have a child placed in their home, or have recently had one placed, and the adoption worker suggests a group that is being run for their benefit, the couple will probably find it compelling to attend. In clinic or physician based support groups, there is often great reluctance for people to express angry feelings about the doctors or the staff.

In conclusion, the infertile couple has an unusual need for counseling, support, and advocacy as they negotiate the difficult steps of investigation, treatment, and possible selection of an alternative. RESOLVE offers valuable services in counseling, referral, and support for people at any point in the infertility situation. We welcome the cooperation and guidance of physicians and helping professonals. When medical expertise and psychosocial support join hands, the infertile couple will have truly comprehensive management.

REFERENCES

Menning, B.E. *Infertility: a guide for the childless couple.* Englewood Cliffs, N.J.: Prentice-Hall, 1977.

Menning, B.E. The infertile couple: a plea for advocacy. *Child Welfare 54* (6), June 1975.

Menning, B.E. The infertile couple, in Burgess A. and Lazare, A., eds. *Community mental health: target populations,* Ch. 7, pp. 104–121, Englewood Cliffs, N.J.: Prentice-Hall, 1976.

Menning, B.E. The emotional needs of infertile couples. *Fertility and Sterility 34* (4), p. 313, Oct. 1980.

Chapter 6

INFERTILITY
Implications for Policy Formulation

Harriet F. Simons[*]

Reproductive freedom has been an important social issue since the 1970s. Ideally, reproductive freedom would be defined as congruence between desired and actual family size. However, most public attention has been focused on excessive fertility. The bearing of unwanted children has been acknowledged as an area of social concern, while the inability to bear wanted children has not. This paper is an attempt to understand such a dichotomy in policy by exploring some of the issues involved in the formulation of policies affecting infertility.

BACKGROUND

An early public response to infertility in this country occurred during the Depression, under the auspices of the American Birth Control League.[1] Ten years after the first birth control

*Research for this article was conducted under a grant from N.I.M.H. (National Institute of Mental Health), "Public Policy Impacts on American Families," Grant :1-T32MH15195-02

clinic opened in 1916, the clinics began to attract infertile patients who hoped that the doctors might be able to solve their fertility problems as well.[2] Over the years some scattered family planning clinics and hospitals have provided infertility services. However, the norm has been for couples to seek treatment from their own doctors, paying out-of-pocket for medical expenses often not covered by health insurance plans. Some areas of the country do not even have specialists certified in this relatively new medical field.

This continual lack in service availability was recognized by the U.S. Department of Health, Education and Welfare (HEW) as it was then known, which in 1975 awarded a demonstration grant to the Planned Parenthood Association of Mohawk Valley (N.Y.) to fund an infertility clinic. The clinic's medical director welcomed the unique award, stating that even in large population centers infertility services were difficult to find. He characterized such services as "inadequate, fragmented and very expensive."[3]

The demonstration program was intended to generate data that would determine the need for infertility clinics.[4] The immediate governmental response to this data was the promulgation of revised family planning guidelines in 1976 which, for the first time, included infertility education and counseling as recommended (but not mandated) components of federally funded family planning programs. The guidelines further stated that such programs should begin to offer infertility diagnosis and treatment as soon as possible. As a first step toward the provision of such services, HEW funded a model workshop on Infertility Education and Counseling.

As a next step HEW in 1978 funded four pilot programs designed to develop "marketable" models for service delivery.[6] These pilot programs, funded under Title X of the Public Health Service Act, consisted of four $100,000 grants to the states of Florida, Massachusetts, Texas, and Utah. In 1980 the Title X guidelines were again revised to mandate the provision of infertility services as part of federally funded family planning programs; however, no additional monies were appropriated for this purpose. To date the change in the Title X regulations appears to have had little impact on the status of infertility services.

The "Invisible Handicap"

While the developments of the last decade have been encouraging, infertility remains a problem that is frequently neglected or minimized. The infertile have been described as "one of the most neglected minority groups in America."[7] One reason for this neglect is the persistence of misconceptions concerning the magnitude of this problem. Many mistakenly believe that infertility is today "almost nonexistent."[8] The recent emphasis on fertility control has served to perpetuate the assumption of fertility. The definition of "family planning" in *The Encyclopedia of Social Work* is predicated on the belief that conception will occur readily when desired: "family planning encompass(es) the basic concepts that it is *possible* to have children when one desires them, that it is *desirable* to conceive children only when one wishes them. . .and that methods for achieving these goals are available."[9] The assumption of fertility implicit in this definition serves to negate infertility as an object of social concern.

One reason that the extent of infertility has been underestimated in the past has been the reluctance of those affected to discuss publicly what they believe to be both a private and a "shameful" matter. The very nature of infertility as an "invisible handicap" makes it easy for the public to overlook its existence. The infertile are neither outwardly disfigured nor do they behave in such a way as to attract public attention. Moreover, the infertile do not pose a financial drain on society that would warrant public attention. There is no costly institutionalization, no unemployment insurance, general relief or disability support to be paid, and no children to become dependent upon society.[10] The lack of visibility of the sizeable infertile population has contributed to the lack of services available to meet the needs of this unrecognized group.

A government report points out that more information on infertility is required in order to determine the need for appropriate medical services as well as to assess the demand for adoption and to estimate the potential effects of infertility on birth rates.[11] Unfortunately, research studies usually focus on an existing area of social concern. Infertility has frequently been overlooked or treated as a "confounding variable" to be controlled rather than as an issue worthy of study in its own right. Some research designs purposely define their samples in such a way as to eliminate childless respondents. Research that includes the childless must confront methodological and design problems: the failure to separate out the voluntarily childless ("child free") from the infertile, the use of anticipated fertility as an indicator of actual future fertility, and the difficulty in comparing data that measures varying degrees of infertility.

THE SOCIAL CONTEXT OF INFERTILITY

Infertility, even when acknowledged as a personal problem, is not always regarded as a social problem. Just as a certain level of unemployment is sometimes seen as "desirable" for the economy, a certain level of infertility has also been viewed as benefiting human ecology. The social concern attending infertility in some ways reflects economic supply and demand. A society plagued with overpopulation might be expected to devalue the problem of infertility or even to view it as functional within the larger context. It has been asserted that infertility, although a vital matter for the couples involved, is "hardly a matter of vital national interest—at least not unless and until the majority of American women are similarly infertile."[12] No one would advocate an increase in infertility as a means of placing the issue on the public agenda. Still, one may speculate that a simultaneous increase in the infertility rate that experts predict and the trend toward voluntary childlessness may result in a societal demand for children. Westoff foresees just such a population decline, which he feels would be dysfunctional for our industrial economy. He predicts that the response to such a decline would be

the promulgation of pronatalist public policies, such as cash al-
lowances for childbearing.[13] Within such a context, infertility
treatment might well assume a higher priority.

The formulation of infertility policies is contingent not only
upon the birth rate, but also upon the perceived social accept-
ability of the problem. One might expect the public and, accordingly, policy makers to respond to infertility with compassion.
However, to the extent that an individual is held responsible for
his misfortune, the sense of obligation on the part of others is
alleviated.[14] Historically, the social attributions for infertility
have been tinged with blame. The original explanation of infertility as divine retribution for sin is reflected in the current attitude that fertility and infertility are the will of God. Women have
traditionally been held responsible for a couple's infertility. Over
the years a woman's lack of fertility has been blamed on excessive luxury, physical work, and intellectual activity.[15] Today psychogenic theories of infertility continue to place the blame on
the woman, often attributing the inability to conceive to latent
sex role conflict. Although numerous studies have refuted such
theories, the idea that infertility is somehow caused by those affected is still widely accepted. These misconceptions "blame the
victim" and can preclude policy intervention by perpetuating
negative attitudes toward the infertile.

THE POLITICAL CONTEXT OF INFERTILITY

Those in need of social benefits must not only prove them-
selve "worthy" of intervention, but ideally their cause should be
one that generates universal support. Policy makers acting in
accordance with their own political motivations tend to avoid
controversial issues. In spite of a resurgence of support for "the
family," infertility treatments to create families have encountered opposition on religious, ethical, economic, and even femi-
nist grounds. Although federal funding for family planning services has gained social acceptance, the initial governmental
intervention in the field of reproduction faced considerable re-
sistance. One barrier to policy formulation has been the belief

that families are private units with which government should not interfere.[16] Birth control and infertility as policy issues have had the added stigma of perceived sexual connotations. One analysis attributes the lag in governmental response in birth control policy (in spite of a generally favorable public attitude toward the subject) to a feeling on the part of public officials that the topic was "fit only for the bedroom and not for the arena of public debate."[17]

The initial political reluctance surrounding the enactment of birth control policy may have been overcome in part by the political rewards inherent in saving (or appearing to save) taxpayers' money. One 1972 estimate claimed that every dollar invested in providing contraception for the poor results in savings of $25 to $70. The savings would undoubtedly be much higher today. No such tangible political rewards exist in infertility policy. The politics of birth control are said to have united diverse factions: "the dollar-conscious, anti-Negro, and humanitarians."[17] The politics of infertility are equally complex. Infertility treatments have been opposed for varying reasons by the Catholic Church, Orthodox Jews, right-to-life forces, feminists, and the dollar conscious. Religious opposition is based on the philosophy that medicine should not interfere with God's will. Right-to-life opposition shares this outlook and, in addition, focuses on the rights of the fertilized ovum, which theoretically might be aborted if treatment does not lead to a normal pregnancy. Even some self-proclaimed feminists who might be expected to support all forms of reproductive choice accuse infertility treatments of perpetuating "the unnecessary view. . .that women's lives are unfulfilled unless they bear children."[18]

Although infertility services have customarily fallen under the family planning umbrella, current funding shortages could set the interests of the "family limiters" into conflict with the needs of the infertile. The provision of infertility services has rarely been a high priority of family planning agencies. Although Title X grantees have been charged with incorporating infertility services into their family planning programs, some fear that the provision of these services has the potential to compromise the programs' initial objectives.[19] A proposed operations guide for family planning programs cites the difficulty of raising staff consciousness to accept the idea "of assisting patients to conceive as well as to contracept. . .An equally difficult hurdle for some may be the idea of assisting low and middle income clients to have children."[19]

CONTROVERSIAL ASPECTS OF INFERTILITY TREATMENT

Infertility treatment for the poor is particularly controversial. Those who would support birth control for the poor from a dollar-saving perspective can be expected to oppose infertility treatment for this group for the same reason. Within the current social and political climate, one might anticipate a negative reaction to the use of public funds to enable low-income women to bear children. One such negative response is as follows: "Federally-supported. . .research and services come to the rescue to overcome. . .infertility. Uncle Sam will, of course, also provide Aid to Dependent Children if the mother is or goes on welfare. How wonderful it is to be infinitely resourceful!"[12] The issue of public funding of infertility treatment raises the question of equal access to health care for the low-income population. Must low-income couples remain childless because they lack the means to pay for proper care? Another equity issue involves the treatment of single women either for fertility problems or for artificial insemination with donor sperm (AID). Although some infertility treatments, such as AID or in vitro fertilization are controversial, one must question the existence of a double standard whereby those paying out-of-pocket may obtain whatever procedures they can afford.

Many ethical and legal questions remain concerning AID even when performed on a married woman at her own expense. Artificial insemination has potential legal ramifications in terms of legitimacy, paternity, inheritance, child support, and adultery (see Chapter 13). The recent trend toward the unsealing of adoption records has long-range implications for children conceived through AID who might seek information about their biological fathers, for donors who have been assured of anonymity, and for the parents who may be threatened by such a revelation. A study published in the *New England Journal of Medicine* raised two main concerns about AID: the need for adequate screening of donors for genetic defects and the possibility of incest as a result of unknown paternity. These findings received much publicity, some of it rather overstated. In fact, the researchers pointed out that while incest is a theoretical possibility "undisclosed paternity as a result of AID may be overshadowed by the amount of unknown paternity in the general population."[20] The article concluded with the following policy recommendations: better genetic screening, a limitation on the number of pregnancies produced by a single donor, and legitimization of the procedure, which would allow for better record-keeping. The current legal ambiguity surrounding AID has led many doctors to safeguard the parents, the offspring, and the donor's confidentiality by purposely keeping incomplete records.

A more recent and even more controversial infertility procedure is *in vitro* fertilization (see Chapter 21). Even before the birth of Louise Brown in England in 1978 made such a procedure a reality, the eminent scientist Dr. James Watson cautioned that the laboratory growth of human embryos could change the nature of the bond between parents and children beyond recognition.[21] In 1972 the American Medical Association called for a moratorium on research into in vitro fertilization. Work on human conception in the test tube was halted in the United States in 1974 on ethical grounds. The Department of Health, Education and Welfare assembled an Ethics Advisory Panel charged with determining whether or not the moratorium should continue. The panel in 1979 recommended that the moratorium be lifted. The first U.S. clinic specializing in this procedure opened at the East Virginia Medical School in Norfolk, Virginia, and was immediately besieged with applications from women with blocked Fallopian tubes. In May, 1981, Drs. Howard and Georgeanna Seegar Jones of the Medical School announced the first American in vitro pregnancy. However, anti-abortion bills, periodically before Congress, which define human life as beginning at conception, would, if passed, imperil further research in this area. The major objections to the procedure center around the possible discarding of fertilized ova in the process of finding one suitable for implantation.[22] The head of the Virginia Society for Human Life opposed the procedure describing it as "a desecration of human life. . .unworthy of a civilized society."[23]

The publicity accorded in vitro fertilization and the latest developments in surrogate mothering have focused public attention on infertility, although, unfortunately, often from a sensational perspective. During the coming decade, the public will be forced to confront policy issues raised by the problem of infertility. As infertility is discussed more openly, the stigma and mythology associated with it should decline, thus minimizing the controversy and blame that have surrounded the issue. As the infertile population becomes more outspoken and visible, they will hopefully be recognized as a constituency worthy of social compassion and political responsiveness to their needs.

REFERENCES

1. Gordon, Linda. *Women's body, women's right.* New York: Viking Press, 1976.

2. Rock, John, & David Loth. *Voluntary parenthood.* New York: Random House, 1949.

3. Nusbaum, Murray. Paper presented at Professional Staff Day, October 16, 1974. St. Louis, Mo.: Planned Parenthood NEDC Papers, 1974.

4. *Syracuse Herald American.* November 7, 1976.

5. RESOLVE Newsletter. September 1978.

6. Interview with Barbara Menning, April 30, 1978, Belmont, Mass.

7. Action for Boston Community Development, Inc. grant proposal. Submitted to the Department of Health, Education and Welfare, 1978.

8. Bane, Mary Jo. *Here to stay.* New York: Basic Books, 1976.

9. Turner, John B., et al. (Ed.) *Encyclopedia of Social Work,* 17th issue, Vol. 1. Washington, D.C.: NASW, 1977.

10. Interview with Barbara Menning, 1978.

11. Reproductive impairments among currently married couples. United States, 1976. *Advance Data from Vital and Health Statistics*, National Center for Health Statistics, Number 55, January 24, 1980.

12. Kass, Leon. Making babies' revisited, *The Public Interest, 54* (Winter 1979).

13. *The Boston Globe.* November 11, 1978.

14. Freidson, Eliot. *The profession of medicine: a study of the sociology of applied knowledge*, New York: Dodd, Mead & Co., 1972.

15. Eversley, D.E.C. *Social theories of fertility and the malthusian debate.* Oxford: Oxford University Press, 1959.

16. Family Impact Seminar. Interim Report. George Washington University, 1978.

17. Dienes, C. Thomas. *Law, politics, and birth control.* Chicago: Univ. of Illinois Press, 1972.

18. *The Boston Globe.* November 29, 1978.

19. Menzel, Trudy and P. Goodstein. "Infertility Operations Guide for Family Planning Programs." 2nd Draft. Boston: JSI, 1980.

20. Curie-Cohen, Martin, et al. Current perspectives on AID in the U.S., *New England Journal of Medicine, 300* (11), March 15, 1979.

21. *The Boston Globe.* July 20, 1974.

22. *Newsweek.* June 29, 1981.

23. *The Wall Street Journal.* January 8, 1980.

Part II

ADOPTION

Chapter 7

INTERNATIONAL ADOPTION

Julie E. Ginsburg

Most of the couples that we see at International Adoptions come to us with their dreams in shambles. They had married assuming they were going to have biological children. To their surprise it did not happen as they had planned. After infertility testing and an agonizing length of time they decide to adopt a child. If the domestic agencies stop laughing at them long enough, however, they tell them that the wait for a healthy Caucasian infant will be from three to eight years. At this point our couple often decides to reevaluate things, and this then is when we see them.

These couples are faced not only with the fact that their fantasies of the families they thought they would have will never be, but also with the fact that if they are going to parent at all they will be parenting a child who will in all probability look very different from them. For many couples this is a very obvious statement about their infertility, which has already caused them a great deal of pain. And now their family will become public property. How many families actually stand out at McDonald's? If you are standing there, however, with a child who looks nothing like you calling you Mommy and Daddy everyone will feel free to ask questions or make comments. It is an invasion of privacy that persists through the years. Five or ten years later when you are enrolling your child in camp or ballet class others will still be pointing out to you the difference in your family unit.

And what about your parents? For the adoptive grandparents it is the loss of the grandchild they assumed they would have. How many grandparent's fantasies include an Eduardo Philipé? Adoption of a foreign child is something they never anticipated. Although most couples say that their parents' feelings and attitudes do not affect them, they do. You have a grandpa, for instance, who, when the child arrives will play with him inside but will not go outside with the child for a walk. Or you have a grandma who is walking down the street with her grandchild for the first time and a neighbor comes over and says, "My goodness, is that the best your daughter could do?" Whereas the adoptive couple themselves have had a chance to sort out many different feelings and attitudes through the home-study process, pre-adoptive groups, or agency workshops, their parents have not. To see their parents hurt, perplexed, and embarrassed has its effect on the adoptive couple as well.

An adoptive family becomes a member of the "supermarket set." Every time you go to the market the community is going to have some kind of statement to make about what you've done and how they feel about it. They may automatically assume that your mate is of a minority race. Or there was the mother who reported that someone had come up to her saying, "Well, your husband was certainly tolerant of your affair, wasn't he?" We have the mother who was standing looking at baby cereals with her infant Korean son and a lady came up behind her saying, "You know, I bet he'd love the rice cereal." There are always the comments too such as, "When your child learns to talk, I bet he'll have an accent." My favorite remark comes from the couple who adopted a two-year-old Korean boy. Their neighbor arrived and looked and looked at the little boy, trying to think of something to say. Finally she said, "You know, I bet his mother was a whore." His adoptive mother said simply, "Well, I bet he won't be." The supermarket syndrome can be wearing and not much fun.

Before a couple applies to our agency they are fairly well prepared for what our agency does, the way we work, and what is involved in the adoptive process. We have a thorough information packet and a fairly long application form. Couples (or single applicants) are asked to write about themselves, their backgrounds, their present circumstances, their strengths, their weaknesses, their marriage, their reasons for wanting to adopt, their feelings about infertility, their experience with children, and their feelings about how their family, friends, and community will react to their adoption of a child who will look so different from themselves. The written material is the focus of our interviews during the home study.

International Adoptions perceives the home study process to be one in which couple and social worker together determine whether it is appropriate for this particular couple to parent the kinds of children that we have available at this particular time. We assume that couples coming to us feel that they would make good parents. Besides, anybody can tell us anything they want and get through the home study process if that is what they are determined to do. On the other hand, we hope that couples will share with us their questions and fears. This makes it easier for us to share with them our experiences with the children who have been adopted and the kinds of difficulties they and their families have gone through. Most of the time we find that by the end of the process if an overseas adoption is not an appropriate choice for a family the couple has made their own decision to withdraw. Very seldom do we and the couple totally disagree as to whether this would be a happy experience for both parents and child.

A large part of the home study process involves peoples' biases, and everyone has some. This is a racist society with a great deal of color consciousness. It is important for the couples to come to terms with where they are on the spectrum. They can tell us that they don't care and that color is not an issue for them. They are the ones, however, not we, who are going to be living with this child, and they are the ones who have to understand what really does make them uncomfortable. Parents who want very young infants from the Latin American countries, for instance, have to realize that although children are often born very light, they do darken as they get older. Interestingly, in the reverse, we have seen some fairly dark-skinned children arrive who have lightened as time has gone by. Thus we want couples to think in terms of a child to whom they can make a life-time commitment. The cute baby stage will pass quickly, and there are many ups and downs ahead. Although it may sound premature before the child has even arrived, we encourage parents to envision themselves as the parents of a demanding two-year-old, klunky nine-year-old, rebellious adolescent, and finally, and equally important, as grandparents.

We try to give parents some educational and emotional preparation for what parenting any child is like. Parenting in and of itself can be very frustrating, in addition to the fact that they will be parents of an adopted child who will be so physically different from themselves. Adoptive parents find it harder to complain about their children. They have waited so long and gone through so much that they feel very guilty saying "I just can't stand that kid—he is driving me wild!" Their family, friends, or community turns to them and says, "Well, why did you do it? You didn't have to" or "I told you so." Adoptive parents can feel very isolated with the conflicting feelings inherent in raising any child.

Many parents judge their success in parenting by how happy their child looks and/or how well he/she does in school. Adoptive parents often fall into the trap of using these same guidelines as a measurement of whether or not their child's adoption is a success. Realistically, every child has periods of frustration. Behavior may range from whiny or angry to totally disruptive. Performance in school may suffer. But the goal is to help one's child cope constructively with these periods, rather than to judge one's success or failure as a parent—and particularly as an adoptive parent. Adoptive parents need to be aware of expecting too much from their child in order to show themselves and others that their adoption is "a success." Conversely, they may expect too little of their child because, "Well, he/she is adopted, you know." Part of the home study process, then, is to help parents understand what the developmental stages are for all children; they can then put their child's behavior into perspective and not confuse every negative action or attitudes with the fact of adoption.

Finally, we deal with a couple's feelings about infertility—the feelings of anger, loss, rejection—the feeling that something is wrong with them—the feeling that they have missed something they had wanted all their lives. Fertility testing is humiliating, and couples often come to the adoptive process feeling degraded and like non-persons. There is sadness and sometimes overwhelming and unbearable pain. Couples keep asking themselves why, why, why? Home studies are unheard of for biological parents. For the adoptive couple the process often heightens their feelings of being inferior and different. The loss of control over this, the most personal part of their lives, can be devastating. In an adoption from overseas in particular, the enormous amount of paper work, the constant delays and uncertainties can make a family's feelings of helplessness all the more difficult to bear. The agency is acutely aware of this, and although we make every effort to be as available and as supportive as possible, we know that until that child comes there is often no way that we can alleviate a couple's anxiety and pain.

Recently there have been children available from Colombia, Brazil, Peru, India, and in small numbers from the Dominican Republic, Guatemala and Chile. Korea has been a very consistent source of children.

A further complication is the fact that India is now the only source where the children are escorted here, rather then having one or both parents fly to the country of the child's birth. Whereas this makes the process much simpler and less expensive, the children are usually darker from India than from any other source. Parents who were hoping for a lighter child often have trouble with this.

In Colombia the stay for the parents is one to two weeks. In Brazil the stay is from two to three weeks, and in Peru the stay can be from four to six weeks. To even comtemplate traveling to and staying in a foreign country for that long can be overwhelming. There is the language problem and concern about how long one can be away from his or her job. And an overseas adoption is very expensive. The cost from application to legal finalization can range from three to six thousand dollars or more. The fact that so much of the money is tied up in transportation, travel expenses, and translations does not make the expense easier to bear. Parents often have difficulty explaining to relatives and friends why an adoption is so expensive if it is not black market—or even why they should have to pay for adoption from these underprivileged and underdeveloped countries at all. Escorts from other countries can be hired.

The age range of the children available is between three months and eleven years. The majority of the couples we see are interested in infants as young as possible, and the majority of the children we place arrive between the ages of six months to one year.

Certainly one of the major concerns adoptive parents have is health—the nutritional diet and prenatal care the biological mother received, the biological parents' medical background, and the quality of physical and emotional care their child has received up until the time of assignment. Unfortunately, these are areas in which we usually have no information. We can only assume that the quality of nutrition and care has been minimal. Many of the theoretical studies that have been done point to a grim or limited prognosis for children who have been deprived in these ways. If the families we see took these studies seriously they would be afraid to apply to us at all. For our part, we do let couples know what we know of the results of the latest research projects that have been done. On the other hand, we make it clear that almost all of the children we have seen have been able to make warm and loving attachments to their parents. Not only have these children been able to respond and to relate, but they have also been bright and alert and very age appropriate in their physical, intellectual, and emotional development within an amazingly short period of time. Our agency was founded in 1974 so there are many years ahead in which we will have a chance to assess how successful the process has been both for the parents and for their children. At the present time, however, I can only say that much of the time what we seem to be seeing is families that seem just right for each other, happy to be struggling with the same issues that are inherent in any family unit.

The home study process at International Adoptions includes the written material by the family submitted at the time of the application, a general information meeting, one or more joint and/or individual meetings with a couple, a home visit, and four evening group meetings with other preadoptive couples. Although the families often feel that they will never survive the evening groups for four weeks in a row, many have found these meetings to be the most valuable part of the process. They provide information and education, as well as an atmosphere in which couples can share their feelings about the process. Differing points of view emerge about many of the issues in adoption, "differentness," and parenting. They become, in effect, support groups to emotionally assist couples as they agonize through the wait for their child, and afterwards give families someone to call to help with the common but unsettling problems of adjustment.

The agency itself is legally responsible for a placement for six months after the child arrives in the United States. During that time there are always at least two post-placement reports required by the courts. After this six-month-period, the adoption may be finalized in court. Following this, we hope to be seen by adoptive families as a resource center. It is, in fact, unusual to have major problems during the first six months of placement except for cases of older children or children with a known medical or emotional problem. We therefore feel it is important to make every effort to keep in contact with the families who want to remain involved so that we can help them with the different times we know might prove more difficult. One of these, for instance, is the point at which the child first goes to school. He/she has probably noticed that he/she looks different from his parents, but as yet it has no meaning for him. When other children start to question him, however, the "differentness" can be much more of an issue.

Around age eight or nine being different in any way can be painful to a child. Being the only child in the class without braces can be a disaster, thus something as obvious as looking different is bound to cause trouble. This may be the first time that children feel any pain about their adoption.

The four-year-old may ask questions such as, "Why did my mother give me away?" or "What did my mother say when she gave me away?" but these questions are not usually accompanied by great pain or sadness. The eight or nine-year-old, on the other hand, feels sad that he/she was not biologically born to his parents so that he/she would not have to contend with the rejection and the feelings of "differentness" that his adoption has caused him. Adoption resurfaces as an issue at adolescence, when a child begins to separate from his parents and come to terms with his/her own identity, and again has great meaning at the point at which the adoptee decides to marry and have children. These are times in a family's life cycle in which we hope to be available to both parents and children to help them sort out their experiences and feelings as well as learning from the material they bring us so that we can better prepare the couples that follow.

People often comment that the families we see must be very different. I am not sure that this is true. But I am impressed with the fact that for them being a family is such a high priority. The couples we see are not just interested in a baby—they really want to parent and to be a part of the whole experience. They have been through enormous trials. There remain feelings about infertility and the loss of a successful biological pregnancy. But they want to move on from that and be parents. As important as career or the development of individual potential may be, what these couples want more than anything else is to be a family unit and to be a part of all of the joys and frustrations that that involves. I am impressed also with the strength of the marital relationships—the sensitivity and respect that so many of the couples have for each other's needs. This willingness to respond and to share creates from the start a warm and supportive environment for the child who will inevitably have some special issues and concerns with time. In a society where families are disintegrating at every turn, it is most rewarding to be a part of the process that helps to bring families together.

References

Anderson, David C. *Children of special value.* New York: St. Martin's Press, 1971.

Doss, Helen. *The family nobody wanted.* New York: Scholastic Book Services, 1971.

Duling, Gretchen. *Adopting Joe: a black Vietnamese child.* Rutland, Vermont: Charles E. Tuttle Company, 1977.

Margolies, Marjorie, & Gruber, Ruth. *They came to stay.* New York: Coward, McCann and Geoghegan, Inc., 1976.

Taylor, Mary. *Intercountry adoption handbook.* Available for $4.00 from Open Door Society of Massachusetts: 600 Washington Street, Boston, Mass. 02111.

Chapter 8

PSYCHOEDUCATIONAL GROUPS FOR ADOPTIVE PARENTS

Tovah Silver Marion

Much professional literature has documented both nationally and cross-culturally[1,2] the psychiatric vulnerability of the adoptee. However, little has been reported regarding efforts to prevent symptomatology in this high-risk population. Thus, although according to the U.S. Children's Bureau[3] about 2 percent of the population consisted of adoptees in 1964 (then four million Americans), documented prevalence rates of emotional vulnerability range from 2.6 to 25 percent.[4,5,6,7] Marion and Hayes report that at the Walden Clinic (outpatient department of the Concord Mental Health Center) adoptees accounted for 15 percent of the child outpatient caseload in 1973. This figure exceeded the high incidence rates reported by other clinics, including Schecter's[8] range of 10 to 13 percent and Tousseing's[9] statistic of 10.9 percent.

CAUSAL EXPLANATIONS FOR VULNERABILITY

Causal factors that account for this disproportionate number of adoptees with mental health problems vary. Some authors suggest that unresolved conflicts are basic to adoptive parent-hood.[10,11,12] Other professionals attribute causality to the (adoptive) parents' damaged sense of self stemming from infertility.[13,14] "The importance to adoption outcome of the mature acceptance of infertility," was confirmed in several studies by Hoopes, Sherman, Lauder, Andrews, and Lower.[15]

NEED FOR PARENT INTERVENTION

Many professionals have concluded that intervention was needed for adoptive parents. As early as 1960 Collier and Campbell[16] described a post-adoption series growing from the experience that pertinent material discussed with adoptive parents during placement was not meaningful until later when faced with the real experience of living with their child. Nemovicher[17] advocated preventive work such as counseling courses for all adoptive parents. Dukette[18] stressed the importance of establishing a true parent-child relationship and suggested that management of the adoption was crucial to the future outcome of this relationship. Tousseing[19] concluded that new techniques were needed to help adoptive parents.

In an evaluation of research findings and their implications for field work, Brieland[19] focused on the shift of emphasis in the field from "evaluation only" of adoptive parents to "enhancement of parental capacity." This parallels Argyris[20] general conceptualization of focusing on "competence acquisition." Starr, Taylor and Taft[21] suggested that certain adult coping patterns seemed to have predictive value for adoptive parent functioning and expressed a need for post-adoption services. Andrews[22] discovered that couples can be helped to ventilate and sort out earlier life experiences and anxieties related to parenting and infertility.

In 1974 Asch and Rubin[23] identified "the adoptive mother reaction" and "the father reaction," among postpartum syndromes that are not often recognized as they are not experienced by the biological mother. Severe disturbances may be experienced by certain vulnerable individuals in response to the stressful role transitions imposed by parenthood. They conclude that awareness of these sequences as variants of postpartum reactions can aid in anticipation and hopefully in prevention of postpartum psychopathology.

Research by Baran, Pannor, and Sorosky[24] stated that "adoptive parents are more educable than had been previously thought. . ." These investigations supported the clinical impression by Marion and Hayes[25] that unique stresses were common to the adoptive parent role, as well as the conviction that a preventive intervention focusing on coping skills was a step forward in services offered to this high-risk group.

Borrowing from Erikson's[26] concept of "critical periods," which have become acknowledged phenomena of adult development, as times when personality shifts appear contingent upon the balance of support and stress experienced during times of crisis or transition, adoptive parenthood may easily be seen as such a period.

To summarize, in the literature reviewed most authors focus on agency practices and public policy or on psychoanalytic formulations of adoptee's fantasies and defenses. Some authors focus on relationships between adoptee's age at time of placement and mental health outcome. There is a paucity of primary prevention efforts with this population. Thus, it seemed timely to develop a time-limited psychoeducational intervention for this high-risk group.

METHOD

While on the staff of Concord Mental Health Center, my colleagues and I became interested in applying principles of primary prevention[27] to the identified high-risk group of adoptive families. The two groups described in this paper were conducted between 1972 and 1973. The author and other colleagues have also used this psychoeducational model for preventive intervention with "first-newborn mothers" groups, and believe it can be used creatively with other groups sharing normal stress related to role-transition problems. Features of the model we developed for adoptive parents are described on the following three levels:

Primary Prevention

An informal psychoeducational group was offered to interested citizens of a ten-town catchment area. Pediatricians, school counselors, preschools, clergy, and local newspapers were informed that a professional team of a psychologist and a psychiatrist were available to meet for a limited number of sessions with parents interested in discussing any issues related to adoption. Two groups ensued, drawing a variety of people with something in common—concern about adoptive children.

Meetings

A pilot series of three meetings was offered as a free public service. Twenty-two people came, including two school counselors working with adoptive parents.

Sessions

A second series of seven sessions was offered the following fall. A core of nine people (two couples and five mothers) attended. This time there was a nominal fee.

Participants were not considered clinic patients. No intake procedure and no clinic files were kept. The major focus of these discussions was on helping parents to separate normal developmental issues from those unique to adoption, and on helping to strengthen their sense of parental competence. (We had clinically observed low self-esteem in adoptive parents and the conflicts in mothering previously reported by Deutsch[10]).

Development of a Psychoeducational Group

Differentiating psychoeducational from clinical therapy groups involved our replacing the "typical" therapeutic contract, including deep probing, with a model that imparted information, shared affect, experience, and support. An important focus was the nature-nurture issue and helping parents to view the issue in complementary perspective. Our model aimed at the learning of specific coping skills[20] as well as at the development of general coping attitudes (for instance, regarding the put-downs of neighbors and relatives, feelings of lack of self-worth particularly regarding parent status, or fears and fantasies about their adoptive children). Thus, our thrust was toward general competence acquisition rather than toward remediating deficits.

DESCRIPTION OF PSYCHOEDUCATIONAL GROUPS

Psychoeducational group intervention is defined here as a modality that focuses on coping strategies in current, past, and anticipated situational discomforts.[28] Such intervention addresses the adult ego, gives relevant educational information, allows group experience and support to be shared, and flexibly allows participants a high measure of control over the group format.

From another perspective the aim is to address and engage the adult egos in the task of helping consolidate the members' identities as parents. Our premise was that these people had not fully consolidated their role transition from non-parent to parent status despite the numbers of years since adopting.

Leaders' efforts to address unconscious material at a conscious level involved flexible use of such techniques as distancing "unpleasant," ego-alien material, by presenting theory relevant to the emotionally charged issue, problem-solving in practical terms, and nonanalytic acceptance of negative feelings.[29]

Members' sophistication, capacity for nurturance, and sensitivity to group process were important factors in determining which issues leaders chose to highlight and which interventions seemed appropriate. Didactic efforts were interwoven with discussion of specific problems and concerns. Members were encouraged to serve as resources for one another and to value their competence as parents. "Myths of motherhood" were replaced by more realistic attitudes about "good enough" mothering.[30]

The educational input seemed to help neutralize the vulnerability to guilt feelings that the group soon found to be a common denominator. It seemed to do this by proving at an ego level to members that, "Joey is having separation problems because that is typical for a boy his age—not because he is adopted or because we did something wrong." Or, "Sally is giving us a hard time because she is struggling with toilet training—not because she is adopted."

To underscore this distinction between a psychoeducational group and a psychotherapy group, rather than exploring and interpreting the source of the participants' guilt feelings (in the unconscious), we attempted to remove an arena where the guilt feelings had been rampant (in the conscious).

The premise that parental identity had not been fully consolidated seemed to have been an accurate one. Many members seemed still unsure of their parenting skills and others still fought hard to be included in the term "parent." One member, the mother of a five-year-old boy, was observed by a neighbor comforting her child after he fell. The neighbor blurted out, "You really are a mother." Our group member asked, "What did you think I've been doing for five years? Babysitting?"

GROUP THEMES

A few topics elicited strong reactions from all participants. In our second group: (a) They had experienced exteme feelings of powerlessness with adoption agencies and remained angry about this. (b) They felt bitter about information withheld by the agencies concerning biological and medical heritage. This was particularly painful in response to routine doctor/dentist questions. (c) Powerlessness and frustration was conveyed when they spoke of their bodies' inability to produce children. (d) Coping skills in using words that define and condition relationships were sought. The threatening words "real mother" and "natural child" were discussed at length. (e) A special vulnerability to guilt was felt as a common denominator, they were concerned with how to deal with these guilt feelings to which they felt particularly vulnerable. Additional issues group members discussed were: (a) How to tell your child he is adopted; (b) How to separate normal developmental issues from those unique to adoption; (c) Adoption considered as "second-best," with "the shame of being barren;" (d) Society's put-downs of "How can you leave your inheritance to a stranger?" (e) Relatives' withholding from or showering the adopted child with gifts; and (f) Incest fantasies about adopted children eventually dating biological siblings.

Three additional but important issues also emerged in our group. These included: (a) Poor mother-daughter relationships of the previous generation; (b) Postpartum depression of adoptive mothers; and (c) *couvade* symptoms, the simulation of various aspects of childbirth, by the father, as[31] described by two adoptive fathers.

Psychodynamics

While these groups focused on coping skills, the psychodynamics that emerged seemed important to share with other professionals. Our hope is that by spelling out one group's unusual psychodynamics, we will provide an impetus for other clinicians to share similar or dissimilar observations or findings. Collectively, we might then reach a more scientific understanding to better enable our combined professional efforts to help this high-risk group. For example, it might be extremely supportive for an adoptive mother to realize that she is not "crazy" to have experienced a postpartum depression and that many adopting mothers do.

A few of the more striking issues are illustrated below:

Low self-esteem due to infertility: This was only shared in later sessions. Two women shared a common "confession." After the respective couples had undergone fertility testing, each woman experienced great relief when told it was she who was infertile and not the husband. Their associations to this seemed to point to the infertility confirming early messages received from their mothers that suggested they were imperfect.

Destructive or problematic mother-daughter relationships of the previous generation were shared by five of the seven mothers in one group, as was anger at lack of support from husbands.

Postpartum depression: It was experienced by several of our adoptive mothers (four of seven in one group). We regard these reports as significant since it points to psychological stress during this role transition period as being an important causative agent of this depression, rather than to the hormonal changes in the puerperium to which it is usually solely ascribed. Asch and Rubin[23] have made this same observation regarding what they call "the adoptive mother reaction."

Couvade symptoms: They were described by two adoptive fathers and one adoptive mother. Interestingly, the men who experienced the *couvade* were the parents that nurtured the young infants for a couple of weeks (while their wives seemed immobilized by depression). It was as if the maternal role had been relegated to these nurturant men. One of them recounted becoming ill with severe cramps and diarrhea for the entire day of his biological daughter's birth. These same symptoms recurred the day the couple brought their infant adopted son home, ten years later. While Asch and Rubin[23] describe "the father reaction" as a postpartum syndrome, we have not found anywhere in the literature reports of *couvade* symptoms in adoptive fathers.

RESULTS

How to tell your child he/she is adopted: Before the end of one series, several participants found suitable occasions to apply what they had gained from the group. One mother found the right moment when she and her child were planting flower seeds and he indicated curiosity about the process.

In the course of our seven-session group, two mothers reported that they had comfortably told their children about adoption. Another said she was gaining such skills and would tell her child soon. Two other families re-discussed adoption with greater feelings of competence. The curious mixture of joy and relief expressed by the group in their exchanges of experiences and feelings suggested that isolated pain had previously existed.

All participants felt the group had offered much needed support that had not been available in other community interventions (including psychotherapy). In the last session an evaluation questionnaire was given to each participant.

Feedback from the members indicated that the most valuable aspects of the service, in order of importance were support, insight, and information.

The ranking of these aspects of service ran counter to our expectations for a psychoeducational group. Perhaps this paradoxical finding was due to the nonthreatening, nonclinical group model.

It is not possible at this point to comment on the short versus long-term effects of this psychoeducational intervention. What we can say is that for one group of people, the most helpful aspect of the service reported was "The emotional support of being with other adoptive parents".

DISCUSSION

Having previously noted clinical vulnerability in adoptive families, a psychoeducational community service aimed at primary prevention was offered. Participants' reports of having discussed adoption with their families comfortably and competently, some for the first time, seemed to justify the conclusion that a special need had been filled.

Because of the small numbers in the groups, we exercise caution in generalizing the psychodynamic impressions. However, the issues seemed important to record for future comparisons in professional work with this population.

Cathartic rage over a variety of issues seemed to have occurred and to have met some common need.

The group's capacity for sharing information, concrete coping skills, emotional support, and unusual psychodynamics indicates that a psychoeducational group is an ideal model for dealing with psychologically vulnerable populations in a community setting.

CONCLUSIONS

1. Adoptive children do come to the attention of mental health facilities and practitioners far out of proportion to their prevalence in the total population.

2. These children and families may be viewed as being "at risk" because of the many societal and familial pressures to which they are subjected, in addition to the confrontation of esteem issues many infertile people face.

3. Another predisposing stress factor is often the abruptness of the unpredictable role transition from non-parent to parent, the stress of parenthood without pregnancy, and the special stresses of establishing that bond.

4. While most new parents experience stress in this role transition period, most of the adoptive parents we have worked with have felt inadequate or shaky in their parenting skills, particularly in limit setting.

5. A need was seen to address the areas of specific coping skills and general coping attitudes in this vulnerable population.

6. An extensive literature review including a computer search[28] that tapped three data banks revealed that very few efforts of a primary prevention nature have been made with adoptive parents.

7. Our psychoeducational model was developed to address and engage adult egos in the task of consolidating the members' identities as parents. Its thrust was toward competence acquisition. In this supportive milieu participants learned new

coping skills and attitudes for use in present and anticipated stressful situations.

8. The participants reported being able successfully to use at home the skills and attitudes they had learned in the group. Thus, we conclude that our psychoeducational format was effective with this particular group.

9. We speculate that this model might be applied to other adoptive parent groups and to populations in stress due to shared role transition problems.

10. Lastly, we conclude that the need for more preventive work with adoptive parents is seen as having paramount priority if more than lip service is to be paid to primary prevention and to helping adoptive families.

11. Returning to reality, who is to pay for preventive services? Third party payments are generally available for conditions of pathology only. Who is there to value and pay for efforts to prevent pathology?

References

1. Lifshitz, M., Baum, R., Balgur, I., & Cohen, C. The impact of the social milieu upon the nature of adoptees' emotional difficulty. *Journal of Marriage and the Family*, February 1975, pp. 221–228.

2. Marion, T.S., & Hayes, A. An updated cross-cultural literature review on adoption: Implications for future interventions. *JSAS Catalog of Selected Documents in Psychology*, Vol. 5, Fall 1975.

3. U.S. Children's Bureau, Division of Research. Psychiatric problems of adopted children, *Child Welfare*, 1964, *43*, 137–139.

4. Herskovitz, H.H., Levine, M., & Spivak, G. Anti-social behavior of adolescents from higher socio-economic groups. *Journal of Nervous and Mental Disorders*, 1959, *129*, 467.

5. Schecter, M.D. Psychoanalytic theory as it relates to adoption. *Scientific Procedings*, 1966, pp. 695–708.

6. Pringle, M.L. Kellmer. *Adoption: Facts and fallacies; A review of research in the United States, Canada, and Great Britain between 1948 and 1965*. London: Longmans, Green and Co., Ltd., 1967.

7. Grob, M. & Singer, J.E. *Adolescent patients in transition: Impact and outcome of psychiatric hospitalization*. New York: Behavioral Publications, 1975.

8. Schecter, M.D. Observations on adopted children. *Archives of General Psychiatry*, July 1960, *3*, 21–32.

9. Toussieng, P. Thoughts regarding the etiology of psychological difficulties in adoptive children. *Child Welfare*, February 1962, pp. 59–65.

10. Deutsch, H. Adoptive mothers. In *The psychology of women (Vol. 2-Motherhood)*. New York: Grune & Stratton, 1945.

11. Livermore, J.B. *Some identification problems with adopted children*. Unpublished paper presented at American Orthopsychiatric Association, New York, March 23–25, 1961. Photocopy at N.B.C.C.C.

12. Bohman, M. A study of adopted children, their background environment and adjustment. *Acta Paediatrica Scandinavica*, 1972, *61*, 90–97.

13. Humphrey, M., & Ounsted, C. Adoptive families referred for psychiatric advice. Part II. The parents. *British Journal of Psychiatry*, 1964, *110*, 549–555.

14. Platt, J.J., Ficher, I., & Silver, M.J. *Infertile couples seeking fertility treatment: Their personality and self-concept characteristics*. Unpublished manuscript, Hahnemann Medical College and Hospital, Philadelphia, Pa., 1971.

15. Hoopes, J.L., Sherman, E.A., Lawder, E.A., Andrews, R.G., & Lower, K.D. *A follow-up study of adoptions (Vol. 2): Post-placement functioning of adopted children*. New York: Child Welfare League of America, Inc., 1965.

16. Collier, C.R., & Campbell, A. A post-adoptive discussion series. *Social Casework*, 1960, *41*, 192–196.

17. Nemovicher, J. *A comparative study of adopted boys and non-adopted boys in respect to specific personality characteristics.* Unpublished doctoral dissertation, New York University, 1959.

18. Dukette, R. Discussion of thoughts regarding etiology of psychological difficulties in adopted children. *Child Welfare*, 1962, *41*, 66–71.

19. Brieland, D. Adoption research: An overview. *Perspectives on adoption research.* New York: Child Welfare League of America, Inc., 1965.

20. Argyris, C. Conditions for competence acquisition and therapy. *Journal of Applied Behavioral Science*, 1968, pp. 147–177.

21. Starr, P., Taylor, D.A., & Taft, R. Early life experiences and adoptive parenting. *Social Casework*, 1970, *51 (8)*, 491–500.

22. Andrews, R.G. Adoption: The resolution of infertility. *Fertility and Sterility*, January 1970, *21*, 73–76.

23. Asch, S.S., & Rubin, L.J. Postpartum reactions: Some unrecognized variations. *American Journal of Psychiatry*, August 1974, *131 (8)*, 870–874.

24. Baran, A., Pannor, R., & Sorosky, A.D. Adoptive parents and the sealed record controversy. *Social Casework*, November 1974, pp. 531–536.

25. Marion, T.S., & Hayes, A. Primary prevention in an adoptive parent group: Theoretical considerations. *JSAS Catalog of Selected Documents in Psychology*, Vol. 5, Fall 1975.

26. Erikson, E.H. *Childhood and society*, revised edition. New York: Norton, 1964.

27. Caplan, G. *Principles of preventive psychiatry.* New York and London: Basic Books Inc., 1964.

28. Marion, T.S., Hayes, A., & Wacks, J. Coping-skills and competence acquisition for adoptive families: A new model. Paper presented at the meeting of the American Association of Psychiatric Services for Children, New Orleans, November, 1975.

29. Marion, T.S., McGloin, A.T., & Jenkins, B. Primary prevention groups for new mothers: A community intervention. Unpublished manuscript, Boston, Ma., 1977.

30. Winnicott, D.W. *The child, the family and the outside world.* London: Penguin Books, 1964.

31. Jessner, L., Weigert, E., & Foy, J.L. The development of parental attitudes during pregnancy. In E.J. Anthony & T. Benedek (eds.) *Parenthood: its psychology and psychopathology.* Boston: Little, Brown, & Co., 1970.

Chapter 9

THE ABSENT PARENT
Emotional Sequelae

Carol Nadelson

"The first person I ever saw who looked like me was my son. He didn't look as all babies do, like Winston Churchill: he looked like me. He had my eyes and my ears, and I couldn't stop looking at him. Hour after hour, I'd hold him up beside my face and we'd peer at each other in the mirror. There could be no doubt about it; he actually looked like me."[1]

Adoption is a complex issue, yet its emotional implications for the adoptee, the adoptive parents, and the mother who surrenders her child are among the most understudied areas in the mental health fields.

It is estimated that there are between three and four million adopted children under the age of 18 in the U.S., about half of whom were adopted by non-relatives. Most of these children resulted from out-of-wedlock pregnancies and had been placed in their homes by social agencies before the child was one year of age.[2]

Emotional Repercussions

There is considerable controversy about whether there are greater numbers of emotional problems that appear later in life in adopted children or in the mothers who gave them up. While there are some data available about the children, there are little about the mothers. Clinical data, impressions obtained from therapists treating these women, suggest that long-term consequences include prolonged grief, depression, and high recidivism.

Most reported studies of adopted children lack methodological vigor. There are problems with sampling, appropriate controls, the subjectivity of impressions, and the tendency to draw conclusions from a few case studies. Thus, there is little substantiated data available. Inspite of these reservations, however, there does appear to be some evidence that adopted children exhibit greater emotional vulnerability, including a higher incidence of personality disorders with antisocial symptoms.[3,4,5] It has been noted that the later the age of adoption the greater the frequency of behavior problems.[6] Some authors have refuted these impressions.

Simon and Sentura relate the problems reported to several factors in the family:[3]

1. Parental feelings about reasons for the inability to have children, with conscious or unconscious anger toward the partner who is seen as responsible.

2. Parental fears about their adequacy as the parents of adopted children, and feelings toward the partner who pressured for adoption.

3. The effect of the entrance of the adopted child into a family, especially since it changes the family equilibrium. The subsequent role of that child as competitor, weapon, or vehicle for the expression of parental feelings and impulses is important.

4. The special child mythology:

    a. The adoptive parent often feels that he/she must be special to make up for the lost biological parents and may overreact to parenting and become anxious about performance. This myth is fostered by elaborate screening procedures for selecting parents, implying that these parents are "chosen."

b. The child must be seen as special to relieve the parents of their guilt and anger about their inability to have a child.

5. The specific identity problems of the child, which include:

a. Concerns about the "badness" of the biological parents and identification with them. Simon and Sentura feel that a depressive core exists because of the early object loss.[3] The prominent fantasy of reunion is an effort to deal with the depression which grows out of the fear of abandonment. The child may feel that he/she could be abandoned again. He/she is thus seen as responsible for the prevention of abandonment.

b. Concerns about being "bad," reflect feelings of inferiority or damage because one was given away. Schecter describes the case of a little girl who felt her mother gave her up for adoption because she wasn't a boy.[8]

c. The presence of two sets of parents, albeit one set exists more in fantasy, makes it more difficult to fuse good and bad images into a workable identification as occurs in the normal developmental process. Instead, it is possible to maintain a set of good and a set of bad parents. In the adolescent, acting out may be an attempt to establish a likeness to the fantasied biological parents. Further, the fantasy of having been kidnapped can lead to anger toward the adoptive parents along with a wish to return to the biologic parents. This fantasy may be intensified if the biologic parents have died, in which case the adoptive child may deny the loss and fail to decathect the lost object.[9]

Sorosky, Baron, and Pannor also emphasize the feelings of inadequacy experienced by the adoptive family because of their inability to become biological parents. The adoptive child as the symbol of infertility or lack of virility may be the vehicle of latent hostility by the adoptive parents toward each other.[10]

Nemovicher conducted one of the only objective studies of adopted children.[11] He used matched sets of children and their classmates and collected data from psychological tests. The areas in which he found significantly more disturbance in the adopted children were in their handling of hostility and in their increased incidence of fearfulness and tension. The American Academy of Pediatrics in 1971 addressed the problem of ego identity development for the adopted child as a somewhat more complex issue than for the natural child.[12] They took up several important points:

1. The period of time the adoptive family waits for a child and then for finalization of adoption is one of anxiety and uncertainty that may inhibit the development of emotional closeness.

2. The possible presence of multiple maternal figures, if there is a time delay, may represent a problem for the development of object ties. In spite of the fact that adoption often occurs earlier in the child's life, the importance of the first few minutes to days has clearly been demonstrated.[13] The presence of unknown parental figures do exist as potential identification figures despite the age of the child at adoption.

3. The specialness of the situation may cause overreaction to child-rearing activities. When, as is not infrequent, the child remains an only child, then the problems of the only child are superimposed on the issues of the adoptive status.

4. At the time of learning about adoption, explanations are difficult. The child may desire to search for more information, causing the parents to fear rejection.

How and When to Tell a Child

There has been much discussion in the literature about how, when, and what to tell a child about his/her adoption. While there is agreement on some points, the major areas of disagreement tend to be how much to tell and when to tell. Schecter and Peller have suggested that the revelation of adoption wait until after the Oedipal period because of the possible problem with resolution of incestuous wishes.[8,14,15] Lawton and Gross feel that since the Oedipal stage is not specifically defined and may extend for some time, the dangers of withholding are greater because the child may learn from others and feel deceived. He/she may also feel that his/her worst fantasies are confirmed if information is withheld.[16]

Greenspan and Fleming feel that although children are told early of the event, other facts, values, or fantasies may emerge when they are older and present difficulties.[17] They cite the example of a seventeen-year-old girl who learned that her biological mother was unwed. She had identified with her adoptive mother, who felt that she was defective and imperfect because she could not produce her own child. When the mother urged her seventeen-year-old adopted daughter to be perfect, this was interpreted as becoming pregnant like her biological mother. These authors feel that during adolescence, adoption can be used negatively in the service of separation or can become part of the identity conflict of the adolescent and increase susceptibility to problems.

Senn and Solnit observe that parents often tell a child about adoption dutifully and uncomfortably, at times explaining more than can be understood.[18] Parents may exaggerate the advantages and distort the circumstances. They advise explaining what the child wants to know, rather than "confessing." In addition, they state that parents often need help with their own feelings and conflicts in order to make a decision about how they should handle their child. Many times, following the revelation, there is a period of anticipatory silence and withdrawal that may make the parents unavailable for the questions and concerns that inevitably arise. In addition, parents frequently insist that this child is exactly like a natural child. This may prevent the expression of negative or conflicted feelings on the part of the child.

One of the tales most commonly told to a child is that he or she was chosen because he or she was the best, most attractive, or least crying baby in the nursery. This story engenders conflict not only because it is directly contradictory to the desire for this child to be like any other, but also because it communicates a set of standards or values the child feels he/she must live up to or risk rejection by the adoptive parents.

Illegitimacy and the Family Romance

Most of those who discuss adoption point to the important and special aspects of the family romance for adopted children. The fantasy is universal, and it plays an important role in identity development. In it, the child doubts that he/she is the natural child of his/her parents and fantasies another set who are generally of greater wealth or power. This fantasy is generally resolved in the adolescent period. Ultimately, the child accepts good and bad, love and hate, and other contradictions and ambiguities as integral and as part of the relationship with the same individuals. When there is, in fact, another set of parents somewhere and these parents are either inferred or assumed to be bad, it may be especially difficult for the child to fuse images in the same way as other children do. The result may be a prolongation of the splitting phase. The child sees him/herself as the "bad seed," the repository of unacceptable values and he/she holds onto this identity.

The Search for the Biological Family

The search for roots and origins as part of identity formation is well recognized. The adopted child also maintains a need to seek his/her ancestry. Although some authors believe that fantasies about origins derive from wishes about the adoptive parents and do not need to be worked out by actually seeking biological parents, others have promoted this approach. In the adopted child the normal development of a "genetic ego" may be replaced by a "hereditary ghost," which may result in an even more intense need to know. Sants feels that the resultant "genealogical bewilderment" leads to a decrease in self-esteem and confused identity because the fact of rejection by the natural parents may be seen either as a punishment for misdeeds or inadequacy or as a result of parental inadequacy and inferiority.[19]

The need for knowledge is often either unrecognized or suppressed by both the adoptive parents and the child. The parents are fearful of rejection, and the child often wants to avoid potential hurt. The recognition of the need to know is handled differently in other cultures. The Hawaiians and Eskimos recognize and relate to two families. In Scotland, any adopted person over the age of seventeen can obtain a copy of his/her original birth certificate.[20]

Baron, Sorosky, and Pannor are among those who have considered the concept of opened adoption, whereby there is the possibility of some relationship with biological parents.[21] They propose that the birth parent(s) meet the adoptive parents, participate in the separation and placement but relinquish legal, moral, and nurturant rights, retaining the right to confirmed contact and knowledge of the child's whereabouts and welfare.

Currently, there are several groups actively involved in aiding adoptees to find their biological parents later in life.[22] Most of the requests they receive are from adults. The results of these searches have been mixed, although more often adoptees experience reunions as positive. In a study reporting 50 adult reunions, Pannor, Sarosky, and Baron reported that 40 adoptees found the experience very satisfying.[21] It is difficult to assess the results of the studies done since the impact of the experience not only varies with the individuals involved but occurs in a societal context of anxiety and disapproval. From a survey of Scottish adults requesting information, Triselotis reports that 60 percent desired a reunion, 37 percent desired further background, and 3 percent had practical reasons like civil service and marriage for their search.[23] Sorosky, Baron, and Pannor reported that nine out of the eleven people they studied who did have a reunion found the experience beneficial to both parties.[24] The authors report that those seeking reunion raised more questions about their mothers than about fathers or siblings. The most frequent questions were:

1. What kind of person was my mother?
2. Why didn't she keep me?
3. Does she ever think about me?
4. Did she have other children?
5. Do I look like her?
6. Are there any hereditary illnesses that run in the family?

In addition, they describe the fact that adoptees report looking in crowds for blood relations, and they point to a frequently expressed fear of committing incest unwittingly.

Clearly, the problem of coping with incestuous wishes and fantasies is complex. It involves both the child and the adoptive parents since the strength of the incest taboo may be perceived as less prohibitive, with less fear of retribution, if it is broken under these circumstances than within a biological relationship.

Counseling in a New Context

Counseling is an important aspects of adoption. It should not end with preadoption counseling since many often unanticipated issues subsequently arise for the adoptive parents, the biological parents, and the child.

Preadoption counseling must primarily focus on the process of decision-making, and it must address maturation and ambivalence. Many of the concerns of biological and adoptive parents have been discussed. However, there are some aspects of adoption which emerge later as developmental or cultural issues that may have a profound effect and may not have been considered previously. These include changes in the attitudes and feelings of individuals as well as societal changes. Thus, if records of adoption were to be opened to adopted children at age 18, as they were recently in Wisconsin, the adopted children could seek their biological parents even though this was not part of the original agreement.[22] This clearly represents a conflict between the adoptees' right to know and the biological parents' right to privacy. In this example, the case came to court and was decided in favor of the right to know. This has important implications, one of which involves the ability of the biological parents to work through the surrender of a child if the possibility of later contact exists. For prospective adoptive parents, the possibility of competing with realistically available parents is important. For the child, conflicting loyalties and splitting of parental images as well as problems around attachments and trust may result. Feelings about adoption are complex and include guilt, fear and anger as well as love and commitment, concerns about rejection and abandonment also recur.[25]

Ongoing and/or intermittent counseling should be available as new issues emerge for each family. Some additional important issues are:

1. The feelings of the biological mother when she has a subsequent pregnancy.
2. The timing and way of sharing information and feelings with a child.
3. Handling divorce with an adopted child.
4. The feelings aroused in the adoptive parents by the desire of the child to seek the biological parents.
5. Helping the child work through the special identity issues.
6. The feelings aroused at the birth of a biological child.

Senn and Solnit raise other questions:[18]

1. The resentment on the part of the parents if the "rescue" doesn't work, and the child does not answer the fantasy need or perform as expected.
2. The feelings of alienation that may occur after the child is told and reacts with profound, albeit transient symptoms.

3. The guilt and uncertainty relative to lack of confidence, or the feeling that the inability to conceive is either the will of God or evidence of wrongdoing.

4. The disappointment if it appears that the motivation for the adoption was either ambivalent or related to other issues such as keeping a marriage together.

They also focus on the importance of the involvement of the grandparents in the resolution of questions about adoption. It is clear that the extended family is involved and that they too must be prepared to face their feelings and concerns in order for the child to become part of the family. The family may harbor the "bad seed" idea, and they may see the parents as defective, and/or they may be concerned about the continuation of the family. In her autobiographical book, Fisher poignantly describes her family's refusal to include her in the inheritance from her adoptive mother.[1]

In the past the reasons given for the need for adoption included the presumption that it was both economically and emotionally difficult for a single parent to rear a child. With the increasing number of single parent families resulting from the high divorce rate, and the movement for adoption by single people, their reasons have been called into question. Single people have adopted many children considered "unadoptable" because of their race, parentage, or a defect, with apparently good results although long-term experience is not available. These changes make it imperative to explore motivation and conflict with great care.

CONCLUSION

It is clear that adoption is an extremely complex issue, and that there is a great need for careful long-term prospective studies of all of those involved, using sample populations that are large enough and that include people from diverse backgrounds.

Available data suggests that adopted children may be more emotionally vulnerable, and that adoptive parents must cope with more complex problems than biological parents. We have identified and considered many of the areas of difficulty; now we turn to a search for ways of facilitating success. This can only come from a more complete understanding of the dimensions of the issues, with corresponding recommendations for existing legal precedent and social guidelines.

REFERENCES

1. Fisher, F. *The search for Anna Fisher*. Greenwich, CT: Fawcett Crest, 1973, p. 36.

2. Department of Health and Human Services, 1980.

3. Simon, N., & Senturia, A. Adoption and psychiatric illness. *American Journal of Psychiatry 122*:858–868, 1966.

4. Schecter, M., et al. Emotional problems in the adoptee. *Archives of General Psychiatry 10*:109–118, 1964.

5. Bodmin, J., Silberstein, R., & Mandell, W. Adopted children brought to child psychiatry clinic. *Archives of General Psychiatry 9*:451–456, 1963.

6. Offord, D., Aponte, M., & Cross, L. Presenting symptomotology of adoptive children. *Archives of General Psychiatry 20*:110–116, 1969.

7. Kadushin, A. A Follow-up study of children adopted when older: criteria of success. *American Journal of Orthopsychiatry 37*:530–539, 1967.

8. Schecter, M.D. Observations on adopted children. *Archives of General Psychiatry 3*:21–32, 1960.

9. Wolfenstein, M. How is mourning possible, R.S. Eissler, et al. (eds.), *The Psychoanalytic Study of the Child*, vol. 21, pp. 93–123, New York: International Universities Press, 1966.

10. Sorosky, A., Baron, A., & Pannor, R. Identity conflict in adoptees. *American Journal of Orthopsychiatry 45*(1):18–27, 1975.

11. Nemovicher, J. Comparative study of adopted boys and non-adopted boys in respect to specific personality characteristics. *Dissertation Abstracts 20*:4722, 1960.

12. American Academy of Pediatrics, Committee on Adoption. Identity development in adopted children. *Pediatrics 47*(5):948–949, 1971.

13. Klaus, M., & Kennell, J. *Maternal-infant bonding*. St. Louis: C.V. Mosby, Co., 1976.

14. Peller, L. About telling the child about his adoption. *Bulletin Philadelphia Association of Psychoanalysis 11*:145–154, 1961.

15. Peller, L. Further comments on adoption. *Bulletin Philadelphia Association of Psychoanalysis 13*:1–14, 1963.

16. Lawton, J. Jr., & Gross, S. Review of psychiatric literature on adopted children. *Archives General Psychiatry 11*:635–644, 1964.

17. Greenspan, B., & Fleming, E. The effect of adoption on adolescent development. Presentation, American Orthopsychiatry Association, Washington, D.C., 1975.

18. Senn, M., & Solnit, A. *Problems in child behavior and development*. Philadelphia: Lea and Febiger, 1968.

19. Sants, H. Genealogical bewilderment in children with substitute parents. *Child Adoption 47*:32–42, 1965.

20. Frisk, M. Identity problems and confused conceptions of the genetic ego in adopted children during adolescence. *Acta Paedo Psychiatreca 31*:6–12, 1964.

21. Sorosky, A., Baron, A., & Pannor, R. The reunion of adoptees and birth relatives. *Journal of Youth and Adolescence 3*(3):195–206, 1974.

22. American Civil Liberties Union. Adoptees fight to know who they are. *Civil Liberties*, 1975.

23. Triseliotis, J. Growing up fostered. *Adoption and Fostering 94:*11–23, 1978.

24. Pannor, R., Sorosky, A., & Baron, A. The effects of the sealed record in adoption. *American Journal of Psychiatry 133*:900–904, 1976.

25. Nadelson, C.C. The emotional aftermath of adoption. *American Family Physician 14*(3):124–127, 1976.

Chapter 10

THE ADOPTIVE PARENTS' EXPERIENCE
A Personal Narrative

Louise Cannon Lazare

This my account of how our family came to be: I am stressing those experiences directly related to adoption, although our day-to-day life tends to resemble any other large family. Current issues have to do with three active adolescents on one end of the age scale, a preschooler on the other, and four school-age children in between.

Families arrive at the decision to adopt by different routes. Infertility is a major reason. Wanting to add to a family without increasing the population or the desire to help homeless children are additional reasons. An adopting couple must wait from three to six years for a healthy white baby (black and mixed racial couples have a shorter wait for a same-race baby), or they may consider alternatives: U.S. born mixed-race babies, babies with physical or intellectual handicaps, school-age children, sibling groups of two or more, or a child from overseas. Our first child was adopted in 1966, and the last of our eight children was adopted in 1976.

My husband, Aaron, and I began to discuss the possibility of adopting when we first became concerned about our difficulty in conceiving a child. I searched out and read every book and article on the subject that I could find, accounts ranging from how to make sure your adopted child is perfect, to Pearl Buck's description of Amerasian children abandoned overseas by their American G.I. fathers.

At this time Aaron was inducted into the Army Medical Corps for a two-year-term, and we moved to a farm in Pennsylvania. We consulted several agencies for information. Some flatly refused to work with us because of our mixed marriage (Aaron is Jewish, I am Episcopalian), some sent form letters explaining that they had two-year waiting lists. We attended a meeting of Welcome House, founded by Pearl Buck, which specialized in the adoption of Korean children. The meeting was exciting and frightening, and we had difficulty in imagining one of the solemn-faced orphanage children as our son or daughter. Ultimately, we decided to work with the Children's Bureau of Delaware and were assigned a social worker. To our surprise we found ourselves on our way. Our homestudy was to be for a healthy white infant.

The Homestudy

Our social worker was straightforward and matter-of-fact. Our first assignment was to tell our families that we were considering adoption. It was a difficult thing to do; we were extremely anxious about facing our families' disappointment in our inability to give them biological grandchildren and were not yet used to discussing our infertility with each other.

Our homestudy consisted of about six interviews and lasted six months. During this time we discussed our feelings about our infertility, our own upbringings, our relationship to each other, our ideas on parenting, and our expectations for our child. Two weeks after the final interview, we were called and asked if we would like to consider a two-week old baby girl of English-Irish-German extraction. The following day, in Delaware, a pair of excited parents-to-be heard a description of their future child's biological family background and the birth parents' reasons for releasing the child. It all sounded good to us, but it was difficult to recall specific details, we did not realize at the time how important it would be for our daughter later on.

Jackie

At the Delaware Children's Bureau we could distinctly hear a baby crying down the corridor and wondered to each other if it were ours. Our daughter's name was to be Jacqueline Frances. We were called in to meet her, and she did indeed turn out to be the crier we had been listening to. A Visiting Nurse dressed her and handed her to me. I felt awkward and clumsy, as though I had never touched a baby before. She looked at me with her unfocused baby gaze, and our fantasy baby flew out the window. This was a stranger, and we were going to have to learn to love each other. She fell asleep on the drive home and I prayed she would stay that way until I got over the feelings of panic I was experiencing. "What have I gotten myself into? I don't know this child at all. How can I be her mother?" Although I felt better by the time we arrived home, the feelings of panic recurred over the next few weeks and have returned with the advent of each child we have since adopted.

Friends and relatives arrived to meet Jackie and admire her blonde, blue-eyed beauty. Aaron's mother came with an enormous wardrobe and took me out to buy a sturdy crib and mattress. One, she said, that would last for the next children (it did). My mother began to sew and stuff all the Winnie-the Pooh characters; Jackie had a complete set by the time she was a year old.

Love began to happen as we took care of her. I began to worry about losing her. As Jackie became more and more a part of us, the fact that she was not yet legally a part of our family began to concern me. We had had to sign a form when we received her acknowledging that the agency was still her legal guardian and could take her back at will. We looked forward to the end of the probationary year.

On adoption day I dressed Jackie up in the new dress and shoes especially picked for the occasion, and we went to court, where we met our lawyer and our social worker from the agency.

The judge was a very courteous old gentleman, who talked to all of us and especially seemed to enjoy talking to Jackie: "Who's this?" "Mummy." "Who's this?" "Daddy." We signed the papers making us a legal family. I turned to my daughter and experienced a feeling so intense it made me dizzy. "You're mine. You're really mine."

When Jackie was a year and a half old, we moved to New Haven and applied at a local agency for a second child. We attended a meeting for prospective adopting couples, and then met with a social worker for a home study update. We have found membership in an adoptive parents' group an invaluable experience. Most groups have a mixture of different kinds of families from different socio-economic groups: families who have adopted children of different races, school-age children, handicapped children, teenagers, and sibling groups. There are single parents, infertile couples, families with a number of biological children. There is almost always a fellow member to call for advice, to help you through the wait before placement, and to listen with understanding to your complaints about your children.

Sam

The agency called one afternoon to ask if we would consider a two week old baby boy, Jewish-Italian-Irish. Two days later we went to pick up Samuel Gray. He reminded me of a little gnome. His jaw was broad and his head slightly pointed with a curl on top. He was wearing a blue stretch suit. I liked him immediately.

Jackie's method of dealing with him was quite ingenious; she acted as agent and intermediary. When I fed him she insisted on sitting on my lap and putting him on *her* lap and holding the bottle.

Sarah

When Sam was eight months old we moved to Brookline, Massachusetts, and joined the Massachusetts adoptive parent group, Families for Interracial Adoption. We went to several meetings on the adoption and raising of mixed-race babies.

Our social worker in Connecticut had told us that we could use her agency for our next adoption, so when Sam was seventeen months old we wrote to say that we would be interested in a mixed-race baby girl as young as possible. Unfortunately, our previous worker had left the agency and we were assigned to a new worker who had had virtually no experience in any kind of adoption.

Our new worker seemed to find it peculiar that we were interested in a child who might have difficulty in finding a home. She began to describe several children and their family backgrounds, stressing all the negatives, from family histories of asthma and diabetes to debilitating neurological disorders and criminal behavior. She considered any child who differed from her standard of perfect, i.e., white, healthy, and with a "pure" family history to be undesirable and dubiously adoptable. The fact that we persisted in requesting such a child made her suspicious of our motives and our sanity.

We approached our families with our decision to adopt a non-white child. After they had a chance to think about it, my parents and sisters seemed to enjoy the idea. Aaron's family was vocally upset—they worried about the effect on Jackie and Sam, on the neighbors, etc.

One afternoon the phone rang. Would we consider a three-month-old baby girl, black-white? Our worker added that she was leaving the agency and wished us good luck.

At the end of the week we drove to Connecticut to pick up Sarah Ethelinde. During our wait for her, we prepared ourselves for a dark-beige skinned child with tight curly hair. The baby presented to us had pale beige skin, short straight hair, and almond eyes. It seemed infuriatingly obvious that our social worker had ignored our expressed wish in placing with us the least black-appearing child available.

A good social worker is important in any adoption home-study; he or she can have enormous impact in determining the success or failure of any non-traditional adoption. At the time we adopted Sarah, transracial adoption of black children by white parents was fairly new. A lot of the trial and error learning that Aaron and I did about raising a black child in an otherwise white family is probably now covered in the homestudy.

Sarah's arrival was very painful to Sam; suddenly he wasn't the baby. He hit her the first time she was put in "his" stroller. Two under-two's was more than I realized it was going to be. Jackie helped out like a trooper. As for the rest of the family, all dubious relatives silenced their objectives the instant Sarah arrived. Gifts were showered on her as they had been on Jackie and Sam. She was initially accepted as grandchild, niece, cousin, because she was our child, but gradually, as relatives came to know her, she became valued for herself.

Sarah, by the way, became darker as she grew older and now sports a striking Afro. A petty triumph over our social worker.

About the time of Sarah's placement, I thought it might be fun to help out in the office of Families for Interracial Adoption. The "office" was actually a desk in the office of the Massachusetts Adoption Resource Exchange (M.A.R.E.). M.A.R.E. was a pioneer in believing and proving that no child is unadoptable. It served as a clearinghouse for children and families who were looking for each other. Photographs of waiting children were pinned up over staff desks.

At this point Families for Interracial Adoption decided to change its name to the Open Door Society, in keeping with our expanding interest in different kinds of adoptions. We had come to realize that adoptive families have something in common no matter what kind of children they have adopted or whether or not they have biological children as well.

As Sarah approached her second birthday, we began to think of our next child. We decided to apply to a local agency, and when our worker at Catholic Charities asked what kind of child we were interested in, we were considerably looser. Black or black-white, a boy, younger than Sarah. We were told of a black boy, eleven-and-a-half months old, who had had a minor orthopedic problem earlier that had completely cleared up. Two days later we went to Boston to pick up Thomas James Bradbury.

Tom

My clearest memory after our arrival at Catholic Charities is of walking down the hall and saying to myself, "Please God, let me like him." We met a motherly looking gray-haired white woman (Tom's foster mother) with a little black boy in a red sunsuit holding onto her and standing as close to her as he possibly could. Aaron and I tried to figure out how to make friends with a little boy who stared at us with deep suspicion. (We learned later that he had lost his first foster mother only six weeks before.) After we had been there for what seemed like hours, and Tom had reluctantly accepted a glass of water from me, I nervously picked up my new son, who immediately began to shriek his terror and grief. He howled wetly all the way back to the car. People on the street stared at us. We put him in the back seat of the car next to Jackie, whom he clutched for dear life. He held on to her and sobbed into her shoulder.

He cried almost constantly for the next few days. He began to respond to the other children (he had been in a foster home with several other children), but remained guarded with Aaron and me. For the next year he woke up regularly at about three A.M. and cried as though in the middle of a nightmare. Until he was almost three, he was fearful and suspicious of strangers. By the time he started kindergarten, however, he had become a friendly, self-confident little boy with positive feelings about himself as a person and a black.

Hien

When Tom was eighteen months old we began to think about our next child. We had been reading about the destruction of families in Vietnam and about abandoned half-American children. We made several inquiries and were referred to Families for Children, an agency based in Montreal. The agency worked with an Australian woman who had founded a nutrition center and orphanage in Saigon called Allambie (the Australian aborigine term for the place you rest before you go home). In addition to providing the best medical services possible, they were committed to the idea that children need families, not institutions, and were therefore active advocates of adoption. Families for Children sent us a long list of documents we would need for a Vietnamese adoption, including income tax statements, power-of-attorney, letters of reference, a copy of our home study, birth and marriage certificates, all duly notarized. Everything was sent in by November 1972. In April 1973 I received a battered manila envelope containing a Vietnamese birth certificate, a letter from an American social worker in Da Nang, and a document signed by the American consul which stated that Pham Thi Hien was being released by her mother to "Dr. and Mrs. Aaron Lazare. . .to be adopted by them and raised as their child." It stated that Hien was the child of a black American soldier, and the mother could not return to her family with a black child. There were also pictures of our daughter.

Hien's pictures showed a solemn, round-faced little girl with curly hair. In two of them she was standing next to a sad-faced Vietnamese woman. The birth certificate stated that she was four years old—Sarah's age. We chose to add the American names Anne Elizabeth.

The paperwork for Hien's American visa took several weeks. We sent money for her air fare. In June we received a letter from her Vietnamese mother asking us to be kind to her daughter and treat her well. The volunteers at the orphanage sent us letters and pictures of Hien and some of Hien's own crayoned art work. Months went by as we waited for the paperwork for Hien's Vietnamese exit visa to be completed, but by Thanksgiving of 1973 we were told that she was due to arrive in New York.

The waiting room at JFK airport was full of expectant parents, some showing pictures of their children. It seemed like hours before the children were cleared through customs, and we all went downstairs to another area to greet them. I recognized Hien immediately from the pictures, and ran to pick her up. A few years later, when talking about this first meeting, Hien said to me, "You know, I almost bit you." She glared at me and pulled away.

She had arrived speaking very little English. I became concerned about her because for a few weeks she rarely made any sound, not even trying to speak Vietnamese. Occasionally she responded with "Ahhhh, Ahhhhh." After about two weeks she began to speak in English, and her sisters taught her to print her name; she began to sign her art work.

All parents of overseas children are warned that it is important to have their children seen as soon as possible by their own pediatrician. Unfortunately, ours was away when Hien arrived, and we saw his colleague, who apparently disapproved of the situation. "No medical history?" He examined her with distaste and repeated several times that he would order a blood test for syphilis.

We were concerned about her physical condition; her muscle tone was poor and she waddled with a crab-like gait. We took her to an orthopedist who guessed that she might have residual polio damage. However, Hien was a determined little girl who followed her brothers and sisters as they climbed on our jungle gym, and by the time our regular pediatrician returned Hien appeared a different child. She is now an avid and graceful gymnast.

Shortly after Hien's arrival we started a scrapbook for her, containing pictures of her Vietnamese mother and herself. We were uncertain about when the time would be most opportune to show her the book, but a couple of months after her arrival, Jackie found the book and showed it to Hien, who displayed the pictures with obvious happiness and pride. The scrapbook is something of great value to her; she has shown it to all her good friends.

By June 1974, Hien was an integral part of our family, and we all went to Camp Abnaki in Vermont (now Camp Sloan of Connecticut). This camp is an important feature in the lives of many adoptive families in New England and Eastern Canada. It is a family camping weekend, sponsored by an affiliation of adoptive family groups (Region I of the North American Council of Adoptable Children). The majority of families in attendance have non-traditional adoptions and look forward to seeing each other again. Parents and children become good friends. It is a very comfortable weekend; no one stares at the children for being different, and no one makes parents feel guilty about their complaints.

Robert and David

Several workers from Families for Children were at Camp Abnaki with their own families that summer of 1974. One of them asked us if we would be interested in two Vietnamese boys. Two at once! I had been reading about the adjustment problems involved in adopting school-age children, and the ideas of going through them with more than one child at a time was a bit scary. What would it be like for the other children to inherit older siblings? We had troubled falling asleep that night, but the next morning we told the worker we were game.

A few weeks later we receive a call; there were two half-brothers, sons of a Vietnamese mother and white American G.I.'s. They had had a little sister who died, and the orphanage was trying to find a family for the boys. We said yes immediately.

We received our first pictures of them in August. There they were, two skinny, knobby-kneed little toughs. One was sticking his tongue out at the photographer. I couldn't decide what I felt about them. Looking at the pictures made me nervous.

Their Vietnamese names were Ly Sam and Kim Son. We decided to add traditional family names: Robert Bridgham to Ly Sam, and David Eben to Kim Son.

Having been through one Vietnamese adoption, we set about this one almost casually. We collected the usual documents, and our agency sent off the home study. In November 1974 we received the documents from Vietnam to use to get the boys American visas. We had been warned that the official Vietnamese documents would list the boys as five and six years of age, as the Vietnamese government was reluctant to grant exit visas to older boys who might be of draft age in a few years.

We received more photographs and information from the orphanage staff. We learned that unlike Hien who retained Hien as her first name the boys had begun to use Robert and David.

Months went by. We began to get uneasy about the war, and then a letter arrived from the orphanage notifying us that the American Embassy had sent the American visas to the wrong agency, the Vietnamese visas had expired, and they would have to start all over again. The newspapers were carrying frightening headlines. Da Nang was overrun and there were horrendous pictures of fleeing refuges. We had the unbearable vision of our two being caught up in the maelstrom and lost to us forever.

We called our senators for help. Together with waiting families across the country (and all our friends and relatives), we wired the President, the State Department, senators and congressmen: Don't forget the children!

On April 4, 1975 we heard on the radio that a planeload of children had crashed on takeoff. It wasn't known which orphanage they were from or if there were any survivors. We waited for news at the home of another waiting family. There we sat and chewed our nails and listened to news bulletins. In the afternoon we heard that all the assigned children from Allambie had been on the plane; it was believed that none had survived.

The kids didn't know how to handle all this. Sam sang loudly, trying to distract everyone; Hien and Tom followed his lead. Sarah kept rubbing my back, and Jackie cut out a heart-shaped card which she decorated with pictures of birds and on which she wrote "Dear Mommy and Daddy, I hope a miracle will come to Robert and David because I really want them."

That night we received a call from the parents of an American man who had been a volunteer at Allambie, to tell us that Robert and David were safe with him in Saigon. I had to put Aaron on the phone to make sure I wasn't hallucinating. Everyone was leaping around like fools, hugging each other. We later learned that the delay in the granting of the Vietnamese exit visas saved our sons' lives, and that our social worker from Montreal would bring the boys from Saigon herself. The next day the Families for Children office called to say that the boys were with her and on their way to Canada. Would we come to Montreal the following evening to receive them?

The Montreal airport was full of expectant parents. After we had milled around for some time, it was announced that parents only were now to go to the gate. When our name was called, Aaron went forward and I readied my camera. What I captured on film was two skinny little boys, David biting his lip and leaning back against Aaron. Robert, unsmiling and wary, walked on ahead.

I gave each of them a kind of awkward hug. The boys pulled out their pictures of us and the family that we had sent them, perhaps their way of checking that we were the right parents. They showed us their school workbooks from Allambie, where they had learned a little English. They told us they were nine (Robert) and eight (David).

We stayed to pick up the boys' passports, and then went to greet Aaron's father and some other relatives. Sam had come with us to the airport, too. On the way we met some Canadian newsmen who wanted to know how we planned to raise these boys. "As best we can," we replied.

When we arrived in Boston there were television cameras and interviewers waiting for us. Newspaper photographers and more television people came to the house. For the most part they were quite pleasant, and all the kids enjoyed their moment in the spotlight, hamming it up. For a time I suspected that Rob and David assumed that this was the way all children came into American families. Sam particularly enjoyed being interviewed for television. When asked his feelings about the new arrivals he announced that he planned to "flush them down the toilet if they're not good." He was disappointed to find this line edited out of the broadcast version of the interview.

Adopting an older child (or two) is an experience for which one can never be totally prepared. It has been compared to marriage. In our case an arranged marriage in which the involved parties meet after the commitment has been made. Hien's adjustment was relatively simple; she was determined to be an equal member of the family. The process with Rob and David was quite different.

In addition to the general chaos natural to a family of two adults, seven children, two cats, and a Labrador Retriever, we now found ourselves contending with seven children who were jockeying each other for position (Jackie now had one older brother, Sam had two) and for the favor of their parents. Our two newest arrivals in particular were busy testing all the limits—we found we had to invent limits we had never considered before. We also had to look for a larger house.

Like Hien, Rob and David had spent their early years with their Vietnamese mother, but she had to work long hours and they spent much time alone or with reluctant relatives. They described going out in the evenings and playing with the street kids all night long. Eventually they were placed in an understaffed orphanage where they soon learned how to escape to the beach, away from tasks and schooling. Coming into a family was very difficult for them. The concepts of sharing equally with peers, accepting adult authority, and obeying family rules came very hard to them. We were strangers. They had learned to get along on their own. There were occasions when they were certain they had made a terrible mistake in coming. There were occasions when we thought so, too.

Parenting children, however they come into a family, is never easy. What makes it possible to get through the tough spots is the love and commitment that parents and children feel toward each other. In the case of Rob and David there was commitment on our part, but in the beginning, no love and very little like on either side. In struggling to build a solid relationship with the boys, Aaron and I learned all sorts of unflattering things about ourselves—like how nasty we could get and how loud I could scream and what vicious thoughts one could harbor toward innocent children. Fortunately for all of us, Aaron and I were able to turn to experienced adoptive parents, a wise social worker, and an understanding child psychologist for advice and support through all the turmoil. The biggest plus for us in making this adoption work was that underneath it all, the boys really wanted to love and be loved. It took a long time for this to become apparent. Even in the beginning David liked to sit on our laps. Hugs and kisses caused him to blush with pleasure and soon he began to respond in kind. Rob held out much longer, but by the end of the first year with us he was smiling and pleasant, but aloof. A year and a half after Rob's arrival, he kissed me for the first time, and I will never forget the pleasure of that experience.

I don't know when the love happened, but they are now as much "our children" as are the others. They gradually became real brothers to the other five. Even Sam, who felt the most displaced, now grudgingly admits that he likes Robert and doesn't mind rooming with him (most of the time).

Naomi

About two years after Rob's and Dave's arrival, we began to consider our eighth and last child. We wanted a younger girl. Our social worker found a five-month-old girl, black-white, healthy, and dark-skinned. Jackie, Sarah, and Hien became very excited about having a baby sister.

We had to wait a week before we could pick up Naomi Janet Trinh Lazare. We needed to replace the baby clothing and equipment we had long since given away. I pulled out my old copy of Dr. Spock, and feeling rather foolish, went to the local market to stock up on baby food.

She was a beautiful, smiling little girl with fluffy brown hair, soft brown skin, bright brown eyes—perfect! She seemed as pleased with us as we were with her.

Having Naomi has been a great treat for us all. She's lively, bright, aggressive, and loving. Older siblings can turn to her for affection when the rest of the world is against them. Jackie, Rob, and David are her godparents. They alternately kiss her and boss her around. Sarah and Hien are her roommates and confidantes; Sam and Tom are her good pals. One of her favorite songs is "You Are My Sunshine," but her version goes "Naomi Sunshine" and that fits her.

THE BIRTHPARENTS

When our children were placed with us, we were given varying amounts of information about their birthparents and background. For Jackie, Sam, and Sarah, we were told a fair amount but we didn't write it down, and aside from some general facts forgot a lot of it. The information was given to us for our benefit in deciding whether or not to accept the particular child, and at the time neither we nor the agency realized how important this information would be to the child him/herself. We were now the parents, all the rest was in the past. In Tom's case the agency policy was to state the race of the parents and nothing else.

Adoption from Vietnam was a different story. We were given Hien's birth mother's name, circumstances, and picture. We had a measure of communication with her. We had not expected this; her grief and pain became very real to us. We became aware that not only was Hien proud of the pictures of her birth mother, but that the others were envious.

We recently received pictures and names of Rob's and Dave's birth parents, and Jackie's agency sent us a very complete background, omitting only the birth parents' names. Things are changing. Many agencies are now willing to act as intermediaries between adult adoptees and birth parents, and some will pass information back and forth while the adopted person is still a child if both adoptive parents and birth parents wish it.

The idea of birth parents is threatening to most new adoptive parents. It is only as the relationship grows and the parent becomes more comfortable with it and as the parents come to see their children as individuals that adoptive parents are able to recognize that each child's biological heritage is very much a part of his/her identity. Having friends who are birth parents of children released for adoption and meeting adopted adults has been very helpful to us in learning to deal with our own children's natural questions and concerns.

CONCLUSION

Basically, having and raising a family through adoption is pretty much the same as it would be through birth. There are a few more facets to be dealt with, birth parents, for example, or the social history of a child who arrives at an age beyond babyhood, but in the main the sources of pleasure, pain, and pride are the same. Each of our children is unique and has his/her special talents. The fact that they are from different genetic pools undoubtedly adds to the group's diversity and makes watching them grow and develop even more exciting. Aaron was once quoted by a newsman as saying that we would continue adopting "until we hit a lemon." Well, we've stopped adopting, eight really is enough, but we've never hit a lemon.

REFERENCES

1) Adoption in General

Children Without Homes, The Report of the Children's Defense Fund. Can be obtained from the Children's Defense Fund, 1520 New Hampshire Ave., N.W., Washington, D.C. 20036

Kirk, H. David. *Shared fate: A theory of adoption and mental health.* New York: The Free Press, 1964.

McNamara, Joan. *The adoption advisor.* New York: Hawthorne Press, 1975. Available in paperback through NACAC; see address below.

Van Why, Elizabeth. *Adoption bibliography and multi-ethnic sourcebook.* Available through NACAC; address below.

2) Special Needs Child Adoption

Blank, Joseph P. *19 steps up the mountain: the story of the DeBolt family.* Philadelphia and New York: J.P. Lippincourt Company, 1976.

Kravik, Patricia, Editor. *Adopting children with special needs.* Available through NACAC; address below.

3) Older Child Adoption

Carney, Ann. *No more here and there.* Available through NACAC; address below.

Jewett, Claudia. *Adopting the older child.* Harvard, Mass.: Harvard Common Press, 1977. Available from NACAC; address below.

Jewett, Claudia. *Parent's guide to adopting the older child.* Available from Open Door Society of Massachusetts: address below.

Kadushin, Alfred. *Adopting older children.* New York: Columbia University Press, 1970.

4) Transracial and International Adoption

Anderson, David C. *Children of special value.* New York: St. Martin's Press, 1971.

Doss, Helen. *The family nobody wanted.* New York: Scholastic Book Services, 1971.

Duling, Gretchen. *Adopting Joe; a black Vietnamese child.* Rutland, Vermont: Charles E. Tuttle Company, 1977.

Ladner, Joyce. *Mixed families.* Garden Press, N.Y.: Anchor Press, 1977. Available through NACAC; address below.

Margolies, Marjorie, & Gruber, Ruth. *They came to stay.* New York: Coward, McGann and Geoghegan, Inc., 1976.

Taylor, Mary. *Intercountry adoption handbook.* Available from Open Door Society of Massachusetts; address below.

The unbroken circle. A collection of writings on international and interracial adoption. Available from OURS, Inc.; address below.

5) Adopted Adults and Birthparents

Lifton, Betty Jean. *Lost and found; the adoption experience.* New York: The Dial Press, 1979.

Sorosky, A., Baran, A., & Pannor, R. *The adoption triangle.* Garden City, New York: Anchor Press/Doubleday 1978.

Triseliotis, John. *In search of origins.* Boston: Beacon Press, 1975.

6) Books for Children

Bunin, Catherine and Sherry. *Is that your sister?* New York: Pantheon Books, 1976. Available from NACAC; see address below.

Livingston, Carole. *Why was I adopted?* Secaucus, New Jersey: Lyle Stuart, Inc., 1978. Available from NACAC; see address below.

Lowry, Lois. *Find a stranger, say goodbye.* Boston: Houghton Mifflin, 1978.

Miles, Mishka. *Aaron's door.* Boston: Little, Brown and Co., 1978.

Silman, Roberta. *Somebody else's child.* New York: Frederick Warne, 1976.

7) Parent Organizations with Newsletters of Broad Interest

NACAC (North American Council on Adoptable Children; an affiliation of groups in the U.S. and Canada), Information and Resource Office, 250 East Blaine, Riverside, California 92507. Membership includes subscription to ADOPTALK. Other publications available are listed above.

Open Door Society of Massachusetts, Inc., 600 Washington St., Boston, Massachusetts, 02111. Membership includes bi-monthly newsletter. Other publications available are listed above.

OURS, Inc., 4711 30th Avenue, So., Minneapolis, MN 55406. Membership includes newsletter. Other publication listed above.

Part III

ARTIFICIAL INSEMINATION BY DONOR (AID)

Chapter 11

MEDICAL ASPECTS OF AID

Isaac Schiff

Artificial insemination by donor (AID) may be indicated for the couple in which the male is unable to produce a pregnancy and the female is presumably fertile. At the Fertility and Endocrine Unit of Brigham and Women's Hospital in Boston, we refer males for urological consultation and evaluate female fertility prior to suggesting AID. If AID is judged to be a possibility, the couple is informed of other options such as pursuing adoption or choosing to remain childless. Many couples are referred to the clinic by other physicians specifically for AID. It is imperative that each couple reach its own decision concerning AID and then assume responsibility for that decision.

FIRST VISIT

On the first visit we insist that both the husband and the wife appear. If the couple is referred to us, the appointment generally takes about an hour or two. The doctor goes over the previous workup done by the referring physician,—namely confirming that the woman's fallopian tubes are patent, that she is ovulating, and that the male is definitely sterile. If we suspect that the male has not been adequately evaluated or treated, we will also have him seen by our own urologist. Once we are fully convinced that the male cannot produce a pregnancy with the best of our diagnostic and therapeutic regimens and that the woman is most probably fertile, we then proceed to AID.

Other factors are discussed on the first visit. The couple is informed that there is no guarantee of pregnancy, the success rate is only 70 percent. We really don't know why there is a failure rate of 20 to 30 percent. We inform them that they have an appointment for a particular day at a particular time, but they may have to wait an hour or two because the donor, for some reason, could not produce a specimen on time. Following the initial evaluation and education by the physician, the couple then discusses further details with the nurse. The woman is given specific information and education on how to take her basal body temperature. This is important because by evaluating the basal body temperature, one is able to determine the best time to do the artificial insemination. Finally, arrangements are made for the couple to meet with our psychiatric social worker. We are not screening couples to decide who would be good parents and who would not. The main reason for seeing the psychiatric social worker is so that pertinent questions may be discussed to ensure that the couple is emotionally and psychologically ready to undergo this procedure. To sum up, on the first visit both partners have seen the doctor. They have been examined, the records have been evaluated, and plans have been made to undergo artificial insemination.

DONORS

In general medical personnel serve as our donors. The reasons we choose them are as follows: (1) we have easy access to them, (2) they are usually sensitive to medical illnesses in their families. (3) medical students or residents or physicians have to be healthy and receive periodic checkups and (4) they understand the importance of the procedure. The donors are married or are involved in stable relationships. Because they have a good rapport with our administrator and the clinic nurse, they are told that if they are concerned about venereal disease in themselves to inform us so that we can culture them. Nevertheless, we routinely culture all specimens every two to four weeks. If the specimen is going to be used at 7:15 A.M., we tell the donor to arrive with it around 7:00 A.M. The donor does not bring the specimen to the clinic but takes it to a prearranged spot elsewhere in the hospital. This is to ensure that no patient be able to identify that person as a donor.

METHOD OF AID

If the patient ovulates on day 12, the best time to do insemination might be days 10 and 12. The inseminations are usually done by the nurse. We certainly allow the husband to be present in the examining room and watch the procedure, if that is the couple's preference. The specimen is taken and examined under the microscope to be sure that it is fertile. A very small portion (0.2 cc) of the ejaculate is placed in the cervical canal after the mucus has been examined for live sperm, SBK (spinnbarkeit), and ferning. An entire specimen is not put inside the cervix because it contains prostaglandins and can produce violent contractions of the uterus. The examining table is adjusted to elevate the woman's hips.

During the days following the procedure, the woman continues to record her basal body temperature. If she does not become pregnant, on the first day of her next menstrual cycle she is asked to mail her temperature chart to us. We go over the chart each month to determine if our timing was appropriate, and thus make the necessary adjustments.

RESULTS

The success rate for any given couple that enters our clinic for AID is about 70 percent and in any given cycle about 15 percent. We stress the fact of this difficulty and that it may take many cycles. Our results suggest that women over 30 have a decreased pregnancy rate as compared with women under 30. For the couples who become pregnant it is a very happy occasion for them as well as for us. For those who do not, we continue to repeat the artificial insemination. After about six months, if there is no pregnancy we reevaluate their condition. We consider doing laparoscopy to rule out other factors in the woman. We rarely do laparoscopy prior to artificial insemination when the tubogram is normal as it involves a risk. After one to one-and-a-half years without success, the chances of future pregnancies are relatively slim. Most of the couples then drop out. We rarely discontinue patients, as we prefer them to make that decision themselves, just as we encourage them to take the responsibility for starting the therapy.

Artificial insemination is a very expensive procedure both financially and emotionally. Recognizing this, we are extremely sensitive to these factors in dealing with our couples. We try to offer them as much support as possible.

REFERENCES

Beck, W.W. Jr. A critical look at the legal, ethical and technical aspects of artificial insemination. *Fertility and Sterility, 27* (1):1–8, Jan. 1976.

Curie-Cohen, M., Luttrell, M.S., & Shapiro, S. Current practice of artificial insemination by donor in the United States. *New England Journal of Medicine, 30,* (11): pp. 585–589, March 15, 1979.

David, A., & Avidon, D. Artificial insemination donor: Clinical and psychological aspects. *Fertility and Sterility, 29* (5):528–532. May 1976.

Dixon, R.E., & Buttram, M. Artificial insemination using donor semen: A review of 171 cases. *Fertility and Sterility, 27* (2):130–134, Feb. 1976.

Shane, J., Schiff, I., & Wilson, E. The infertile couple. *Ciba Clinical Symposia. 28* (5): 1976.

Chapter 12

THE ROLE OF
THE NURSE IN AID

Sharon Gibbons Collotta

Prior to instituting artificial insemination our couples at the Brigham and Women's Hospital, formerly the Boston Hospital for Women, have an appointment for a general discussion. At this time the nurse discusses with them the costs and the logistics of artificial insemination. Specifically, she explains how the specimen is brought into a centrally located area outside the unit and how the appointment is coordinated with ovulation by keeping basal body temperature charts. The importance of accurate basal body temperature charting by the woman is stressed, as is an explanation of how matching of the donor takes place. We make an effort to match the donor to the recipient couples.

Of course race is matched. Blood type is selected so the husband is not excluded as the biologic father of the child by blood typing. Eye color and hair color are also matched. During the general discussion of the issues of artificial insemination we stress the confidentiality and the anonymity maintained for the couple and for the donor. We have a coded record-keeping system that maintains strict anonymity for the couple. There is absolutely no way that anyone can determine, outside of the clinic personnel, that they are having artificial insemination. At this

133

time we explain the legal consent form that the couple is asked to sign. The consent form states that they have full knowledge and information about artificial insemination and that they are both willingly participating in this project, that there is no guarantee of success, and that they agree to remain anonymous and not try to find out the donor's identity. I also tell the couple about the screening procedure of our donors. The donors have complete physical exams. Any donor with any medical problems would be excluded from our donor pool. They are proven fertile by a good quality semen analysis.

When the couple does come in for the insemination, they find it to be a technically simple, painless procedure. I feel that the most important aspect of care for our patients is not the technical aspect but the continuity and emotional support provided.

Artificial insemination, first of all, is a very difficult regime to undergo emotionally. It seems to pervade all aspects of the couple's lives. It takes tremendous emotional strength to come in for the insemination month after month if they have repeated failures. All our couples feel ambivalent about artificial insemination and would not be there having AID if they didn't have to be. I think the ambivalences need to be discussed and addressed and not ignored. After the insemination, the woman remains on the table with her hips elevated for about twenty minutes. This provides an excellent opportunity to get to know the couples very well. The nurse stays with them during this time to discuss their frustrations at having failed the previous month, their anticipation this month, the problems that they may encounter, getting off from work, and so on. Both partners are usually employed. It is extremely difficult to get out of work two or three times during any given week to come in for insemination. They must provide some sort of excuse to their employers, or if it is on a Saturday or Sunday morning they must perhaps provide excuses to their family and friends as to where they are going at seven o'clock in the morning. This is quite anxiety provoking for them.

They utilize the nurse as a sounding board to vocalize their frustrations and their anger. They do feel angry, and this anger is sometimes directed towards their spouse. We have conducted several support groups for our artificial insemination patients run by our nurse and social worker. Throughout these support groups it became evident that artificial insemination was emotionally taxing. Our patients found it extremely helpful to speak to others having the same experience with AID about their problems and frustrations. We tried to get a couples group together but did not have a quorum of couples; we eventually did have a woman's group, where the women receiving artificial insemination participated. They discussed problems and feelings that they experienced with other women also receiving artificial insemination. This provided a unique forum for them to meet other women in their situation.

I'd like to tell you about some of the most common problems and the most common topics discussed during these support groups. Pregnancy is a very sensitive issue for these women. One frequently discussed topic was that of siblings or friends achieving pregnancies and having to maintain a close relationship with them. They described how painful it was for them to endure this relationship and how really jealous they were of their siblings or friends who had achieved a pregnancy. They discussed telling others about artificial insemination. Most of our couples do not tell other people about it. Some do tell their parents. They seem to feel the need to have parental consent and approval to go ahead with this procedure. Most of our couples who have told their parents received support and acceptance from them. Very few couples tell anyone else. We had one couple who told many friends about it and were sorry they did so. Once they achieved a pregnancy the problem arose of when and how to tell their children about artificial insemination. When discussion of this subject cannot take place freely, to whom can you turn for support and encouragement? They need people to talk to during the months of artificial insemination. There seems to be an almost chronic depression that these couples go through during the months of artificial insemination; it is a cyclic depression. They experience depression around the time of their menstrual periods, they pick up a little when they come in for insemination, and their anticipation and anxiety is heightened during the two weeks after the insemination when they might be pregnant and are waiting for their periods. It is a very difficult regime to endure without anyone to talk to about this from whom they can receive support.

Another very commonly discussed problem was that of advancing age. Most of our patients seemed to be in their thirties. It is well known that fertility rates decrease after 30 or 35 and this is a source of tremendous anger and frustration as the months pass. Our couples feel out of control and they do indeed have no control over advancing age. As time passes they are getting older and their fertility is decreasing.

Another commonly discussed topic is that of female fertility. Am I fertile? Why haven't I conceived? Should I go on for further expensive testing? Should I come in for a laparoscopy and undergo general anesthesia? Shall I continue with inseminations? Is it really going to work? It is frustrating not knowing why a conception hasn't occured during a particular month, particularly when timing was excellent and the cervical mucus was receptive to sperm. The feeling of not having control is again extremely frustrating. Our female patients also discuss the need to protect and shelter their husbands from having others discover his sterility. They frequently seem to take the brunt of their infertility problem. They tell people that it is their problem rather than their husband's, yet they feel angry that they have done so. They seem to feel that it is easier for them to take the blame than to place it with their husbands. Having to come in for this procedure is anger provoking. It is costly and time consuming for the female, and she is the one to make the excuses for her absences at work.

I must say that most of our husbands do come with their wives. They come into the room during the insemination or after it is completed, and I think this is tremendously supportive for the wives. It is supportive, too, for the husband because he understands what his wife is going through. He probably feels tremendous guilt. I think a lot of feelings are brought out into the open when they are together and we have been able to talk about things together. We talked about the timing and the cervical mucus and the months that have elapsed since they began artificial insemination. When conception does occur with our patients, they are referred to private physicians. We do not follow our patients once they do conceive. I think it is important that we sit down with our couples before they leave us to begin their care with an obstetrician because it is helpful for them to know what to expect in the future, and what they can anticipate during this pregnancy. This pregnancy is a bit different from an ordinary pregnancy, and I think it is helpful for them to be given some anticipatory guidance.

There are normally a lot of fears and fantasies during pregnancy. Will our baby be normal? Will our baby be healthy? A pregnancy by artificial insemination has added fears and fantasies. What will the baby look like? Will he/she be musically inclined? Will he/she be short? What did the donor look like? Will my baby have brown eyes like us? Will he/she have curly hair? Will he/she have straight hair? These questions come up over and over again with the couple during their pregnancy. These are normal questions and the couple needs to know that they are normal questions. Once the baby is born they will hear people saying, "Oh, your baby looks just like your husband," or "He has your husbands eyes." The couple should be prepared for these experiences so that they know how to handle them. When the couple goes to the obstetrician for the first time, a medical history is usually taken on both prospective parents. If the obstetrician starts firing questions very rapidly to the husband about his medical history, the husband may inadvertently blurt out that this is a child by artificial insemination, and he may not have really wanted to do so. It is important that they come in to us for one last visit to talk about some of the situations they might experience.

In closing, I can only say that artificial insemination is an extremely difficult experience. Yet I think our couples receive good care with us because of the guidance and support offered to them during the months of artificial insemination as well as the anticipatory guidance they receive prior to leaving us.

REFERENCE

Gilbert, Sarita. Artificial insemination. *The American Journal of Nursing,* pp. 259–260, February 1976.

Chapter 13

LEGAL IMPLICATIONS OF AID

Harvey W. Freishtat

When I was first asked to discuss AID from a legal perspective, I thought of the story about another panel discussion that took place some time ago involving an architect, a physician, and a lawyer. They were discussing which was the first profession on earth—the original profession. The architect stood up first and said, "Ladies and gentlemen, there is no question which was the first profession on earth, it says so right in *Genesis*. Who do you think created Eve? It took an architect, one with superb drafting skills, to fashion Eve out of Adam's rib." At that point the physician got up and said, "But ladies and gentlemen, who do you think created Adam? It took a physician, one with great medical, biomedical, and surgical skills to fashion healthy man out of total chaos." Finally, the lawyer rose, and looking rather sagely out at his audience said, "But ladies and gentlemen, who do you think created the chaos?"

It is unfortunate but true that the current legal status of AID is still little short of chaotic. One of the court decisions most often referred to in the AID area, for example, is the Illinois case where the Court announced that AID was "contrary to public policy and good morals and constitutes adultery on the part of the mother." *Doornbos v. Doornbos,* No. 54 S. 14, 981 (Superior Ct. Cook County, Ill. December 13, 1954) reprinted in part in 23 U.S.L.W. 2308 (1954), appeal dismissed, 12 Ill. App. 2d 473, 139 N.E.2d 844 (1956). In this case, even though the husband had fully consented to the AID procedure, the court believed that AID, like adultery, involved "the surrender of one's reproductive facilities," to someone other than one's spouse. It did not seem to matter to the court that the person performing the insemination was a licensed physician, quite possibly female, or that at the time of the inseminating act, the donor could have been hundreds of miles away or even dead. AID was adultery, plain and simple.

Lest you think this represents a singular opinion from a single court, the same type of pronouncement has appeared in judicial decisions in at least one other state[1] and other countries as well.[2] While more recent judicial decision have come to regard the analogy between AID and adultery as "patently absurd," (*People v. Sorenson,* 66 Cal. Rptr. 7, 437, P.2d 499 [Cal. 1968]),[3] few states have straightforwardly addressed the question of any criminal implications of AID, thereby still leaving the matter open to question. It should be noted, however, that many states, including Massachusetts, have defined the crime of adultery in such a manner as to require an explicit act of sexual intercourse, so that the prospects for criminal prosecution of AID donees, donors, or physicians would appear highly unlikely.

It is on the civil side of the court docket that most of the AID issues are arising. Particularly in situations where the marriage has broken down—divorce, annulment, custody, child support—one finds cases where one or the other party is attempting to use the fact of AID to advantage. Typical examples are cases in which a husband does not want to continue to make child support payments for an AID child, or in which a wife seeks sole custody of the AID child and a court order denying visitation by her husband, or in which a wife claims as grounds for divorce that the husband was unable to consummate the marriage while the husband cross-claims that the wife was an adulteress through AID. These are the kinds of cases that continue to occur, primarily because there is still little statutory law on the subject of AID.

Only fourteen states at last count—Alaska, Arkansas, California, Florida, Georgia, Kansas, Louisiana, New York, North Carolina, Oklahoma, Oregon, Texas, Virginia, and Washington—have enacted laws formally legitimizing AID as a medical procedure and legitimizing the status of AID children. The hope apparently is that by keeping AID off the books, under wraps, and in the closet, the issue will take care of itself. What is happening instead is that AID does keep cropping up in the court reports, but often in unusual and inappropriate ways.

The issue of the legitimacy of an AID child is illustrative. In the majority of states without any statutes on the subject, there is still the common law notion that any child born in wedlock is presumed to be legitimate.[4] However, this presumption can be rebutted by scientific proof that the husband could not have been the biological father of the child. While physicians will often match the blood types of husband and donor or mix their semen in order to prevent just such a situation, court cases are being brought claiming complete sterility or impotency on the part of the husband or utilizing the ever more sophisticated technology of blood testing to demonstrate conclusively that the child is not "legitimate."

Illegitimacy, of course, is itself a most unfortunate stigma, psychologically and emotionally. In many states, moreover, there are adverse legal implications that result from the determination of illegitimacy. For example, illegitimate children may have no rights of inheritance from any man other than their biological father unless through the explicit provisions of a will. If an AID father dies without a will in one of those states, the AID child could be barred by law from an inheritance, even if it is clear that the AID father would have wanted the child to inherit had he taken the trouble to execute a will. (See, e.g. *Labine v. Vincent*, 401 U.S. 532 [1971].) The question of support obligations for an AID child may also turn on the issue of illegitimacy, particularly if there is some question of the husband's consent to the AID procedure. (See, e.g. *Gursky v. Gursky*, 242 NYS2d 406, 39 Misc. 2d 1083 [Sup. Ct., 1963] [child born through AID with husband's consent is illegitimate, but husband is still liable for its support on grounds of implied contract of equitable estoppel].)

What is needed, I would suggest, is a rather simple piece of legislation (drafted by the Conference of Commissioners on Uniform State Laws or otherwise) that would establish conclusively that a child born of consenting AID spouses is the legitimate child of both spouses. Such a law would not only relieve court dockets of unnecessary, frivolous, and often emotionally devastating litigation, but would also be of enormous benefit to the interests of the AID child.

Clarifying legislation would also be very helpful to physicians and other health professionals in the discharge of their own legal responsibilities in the AID area. For example, in Massachusetts and many other states, the law requires that a birth certificate be filled out within twenty-four hours after the birth of a child, and that the form include the name of both parents except where the child was known not to be the product of marital conception. In this latter case, the law specifically bars the entry of the name of the biological father or any other name. Thus, where the attending obstetrician knows of the birth of an AID child, it is technically illegal for him/her to enter the name of either the husband or the donor as biological father. On the other hand, for the physician not to enter some paternal name on the form is immediately to brand the child as illegitimate, thereby making it more likely that the child will find out about its AID origins in an inappropriate and emotionally damaging manner; it also increases the likelihood of future social stigmatization.

What has been the response to this legally created conundrum? In cases where the physician involved in the AID procedure is not the physician attending at birth, the attending physician generally does not know about the AID procedure and hence is not committing a knowing violation of law in entering the name of the husband on the birth certificate. The problem is often dealt with by maintaining a clear division of responsibilities between the AID physician, and the physician attending at birth who fills out the birth certificate. In some hospitals it is clinical policy to use different physicians. In other cases, physicians mix the husband's semen with the semen of the donor to allow for some good faith possibility that the husband could be the biological father of the child. The problem with this approach, however, is that one of the standard clinical indications for AID is that the husband is sterile and cannot produce a child. Physicians apparently are deciding that any damage caused through entering the husband's name on the birth certificate is far outweighed by the damage of not doing so, and they are willing to commit a technical violation of law.

Is there a legal risk in doing this? Of course. But such is the difficult choice now being imposed upon physicians by the current requirements of the law in many states. A number of legal issues are very important in the area of AID. The matter of adequate record-keeping is essential. Part of the mentality of keeping AID in the closet has been reflected in the fact that some physicians, and I suspect particularly physicians performing AID in their offices, are not keeping adequate or sometimes any records of the AID procedure. In my view this is a mistake. It is very important to keep records, in fact very careful records, of AID. Without records, the physician is vulnerable in the event of litigation or any other situation where authorized request is made to review the history of the case—whether by the courts, other government agencies, health care professionals, the parents, the child, or others. While there have been no reported court cases yet, it is foreseeable that cases will arise involving alleged physician negligence in the selection of a donor, in the collection of the semen, in the performance of AID, or even simply cases where there is need to trace the donor for genetic counselling or other bona fide medical reasons. In each of these cases, it will be important for the AID physician to have maintained careful documentation that, among other things, a complete medical history of the donor was taken including a thorough genetic history, that the donor was advised on how to extract the semen and how to maintain and present it to the physician, that the physician was careful to consider compatibility of blood types, and other similar medical information. Without records it will be difficult to reconstruct the situation.

Careful records would also serve another useful purpose in

the event that AID parents become concerned about the medical condition of their child. By recourse to the records, the physician may be able to provide them with valuable information relative to the medical history of the donor without in any way jeopardizing the donor's privacy. In stressing the importance of adequate records, I am not at all minimizing the importance of establishing rigorous procedures so that the records will at all times remain confidential, secure, and beyond the reach of unauthorized persons. However, not to keep records at all is not an appropriate solution to the problem of maintaining confidentiality and privacy.

Another important legal issue in the AID area is the matter of securing the complete and informed consent of all parties involved in the process. Some form of written agreement is advisable, particularly because the law in this area is so vague and because each of the parties in the absence of agreement could be imputed to have multiple and oftentimes conflicting rights and responsibilities. The parents' consent should result from a complete explanation by the physician of what the AID procedure consists of, including its foreseeable benefits and risks as well as possible alternatives to it. This explanation should be documented in a separate consent form or at the very least in the medical chart. The consent should also document the parents' agreement not to seek out the identity of the donor.

The donor should also consent to the process, again preferably in a formal document whereby he agrees that his semen may be used for AID purposes, and that he will not seek out the identity of the parents. The donor should also verify in writing the accuracy of the medical and genetic information he has provided and the sterility of the collection procedures he has employed. The donor should also be specifically assured of the continued confidentiality of his identity from the parents. Perhaps even the donor's wife should be asked to consent to a waiver of any rights she may have to seek out the identity of the AID parents or to bring any type of legal action claiming alienation of affection or similar grounds.

Let me conclude by suggesting that while the law may not have played a very constructive role in the AID process to date, one thing it has done is to leave matters largely to the discretion and best judgment of the family and health care professionals involved. The key from the point of view of health care professionals is to be aware of the implications of AID—medical, emotional, and legal—and then to act on the basis of one's best clinical judgment. If that is done, the law, even in its present state, will hopefully not be a major obstacle.

REFERENCES

1. *Gursky v. Gursky,* 39 Misc. 2d 1083, 242 N.Y.S. 2nd 406 (Sup. Ct. 1963).

2. *Orford v. Orford,* 49 Ont. L.T. 15, 18, 58 D.L.R. 251, 253-4 (1921).

3. See also *MacLennan v. MacLennan,* [1958] Sess. Cas. 105, [1958] Scots L.T.R. 12 (Sess. Ct. Outer House).

4. See, e.g. *Kusior v. Silver,* 54 Cal. 2d 603, 354 P. 2d 657 (1960).

Chapter 14

PSYCHOLOGICAL ASPECTS OF AID

Malkah T. Notman

Artificial insemination by donors has offered an immensely helpful resource for infertile couples. This is particularly important where the infertility problem is largely the man's, for couples who have genetic problems transmitted through the father, or where because of the genetic combination of mother and father a latent hereditary problem might surface.

The decision to choose artificial insemination is a complicated one. For some couples there is the guarantee that at least there is one biological parent rather than completely unknown parentage. On the other hand, some couples prefer the "equality" implicit in adopting a child. For some couples the experience of pregnancy is important. This is particularly true where the man is infertile, and usually not so important where there has been one successful pregnancy. Artificial insemination and pregnancy is also sometimes chosen because it permits the couple a period of adaptation to the pregnancy and the maturational processes that go on during that time; this is different from the rather sudden confrontation with a new baby, which may occur when one adopts. As with adoption this is not an easy decision to reach, although more difficult for some people than for others.

It represents a confrontation for the couple with their infertility (a problem discussed more fully elsewhere in this book). It is particularly difficult for some men to deal with their infertility, just as it is for some women; others may adapt more easily to the situation. However, some sense of loss or defect is probably universal. It affects the sense of masculinity and pride in being able to carry through the fathering of a child. If the man is infertile he is differentially affected if the wife then goes through a pregnancy. Unlike a couple that adopts, where both are in an equal position in relation to the child, the woman does have the intimate experience of the pregnancy and the father is potentially more remote and more shut out. This creates the possibility for a very different relationship to the pregnancy and the child. Nevertheless, it can offer the couple an approximation of an ordinary pregnancy and delivery.

For some men the choice of artificial insemination is a very positive one. It represents a support of the wife's pregnancy and the recognition and willingness to participate in this somewhat unequal experience. It is of course possible to have many feelings at the same time. For many some of the deeper feelings go unrecognized for some time. Sometimes they are displaced onto other aspects of the experience. At other times they remain buried for a very long time. The couple that comes to this decision has usually had a number of experiences and failures in other directions.

Another very positive aspect to this decision derives from the feeling that something *can* be done, that one can get around a particular problem, whether it is infertility or genetic and that there really is a way out. This can provide enormous relief from some aspects of the crisis created by infertility. It does, however, have an emotional cost and a great deal of stress associated with it. This stress can be manifest in a variety of ways, for example, uncertainty about the decision, or later on during the pregnancy, in worries about the pregnancy or even after the baby has been born such as concerns about the baby's appearance and resemblance to the father. The stress can emerge in apparently unrelated ways. Marital problems may develop. If the couple separates, legal complications may ensue with the father's challenging the paternity of the child. Other issues may surface that may not be consciously connected by the couple with the underlying tensions about the infertility or the concern about the paternity of the baby. They may nevertheless be related. Sometimes concerns are expressed indirectly, such as by worrying about what other people will think about the baby or what grandparents will think. Many people feel reluctant to reveal that this baby is an artificial insemination baby. They anticipate a negative reaction from grandparents if they are to feel that there is a "stranger in the act," someone not part of the family. They may wonder how the baby will be judged by other people. The legal ambiguities of the status of the baby certainly do not help. The explicit accusations of adultery that have been raised or the question of who has legal responsibility for fathering the child other than the spouse of the woman carrying the pregnancy really play into the anxieties and fantasies of the individuals involved and contribute to the stress.

The procedure itself also holds some inherent stresses. In many settings there are very few supports available. The setting and the way in which the procedure is done is extremely important. Both men and women are sensitive to subtle nuances in a situation involving reproduction. This is also true of any pregnancy, in which both parents are very responsive to interactions with their obstetrician or with the office staff, and are very quick to perceive criticism or a sense that something is not going well. This can be heightened where artificial insemination has occurred. Since artificial insemination is a situation that is not "normal," anything that seems to be going wrong is very anxiety provoking, and under these circumstances one might consider hypersensitivity to be normal. Sometimes the husband is asked to come in to the clinic or the hospital with his wife when the insemination is performed. Many times, however, he is not, and the procedure is carried out as if it were a strictly medical procedure, minimizing and often ignoring the emotional aspects. The woman usually takes the sole responsibility for making the appointment and often has to spend a lot of time alone in the clinic waiting for a period after the sperm has been inserted. She really bears the brunt of the uncertainty as well as the mechanical aspects of the procedure and sometimes feels some resentment that she has to "go it alone even though it's not her fault." Since much of the workup may not involve complicated procedures, physicians are sometimes very matter-of-fact about it. Women who are not adequately supported may feel very resentful, but may have considerable difficulty in expressing this resentment. They may resent the professional, distant manner of those carrying out the procedure as well as the non-humanness and the lack of support.

Because of some of the potential legal problems as well as the emotional ones, there is concern about not revealing who the donor is. However, most participants have many fantasies, conscious and unconscious, about the donor of the sperm. They are told something about the person, namely, that there is an attempt to match the physical characteristics with those of the parents. Where there have been genetic problems, the parents know that these will be avoided in the selection of the donor. Medical students and house staff are often used, presumably because they can give a good medical history about their own backgrounds and are available at the place where the insemination is performed. Participants in AID often feel that this is a way of selecting good genetic stock, so to speak, because these are men who have the capacity to progress academically.

There are also many normal fantasies connected with the procedure. There are frequently fantasies about the donor. The woman may feel that he is a very special person or have some specific ideas about who he is. Some people fantasize that the sperm somehow got mixed up, and someone other than the selected donor became the actual donor. The mix-up may be felt to be either deliberate or accidental, and the fantasied donor may be "better" or "worse."

There is also a great deal of concern about keeping the procedure confidential. Some may worry about names appearing on hospital charts. Some report experiences of seeing their names in a list of patients scheduled on a given day at a clinic.

They then fear that this list is available to the public and that this very personal secret will be revealed.

Another way in which the experience can become unrealistically perceived is a sense that the procedure is in some way analogous to a rape; that is, the woman feels coerced or feels that she participates impersonally in a sexual experience. The impersonality and the clinical context in which the sperm is received stimulates these feelings.

The concerns of the husbands are also considerable. They share the strong feeling that confidentiality should be preserved; they also are prone to fantasies and competitive feelings about the donor. There is usually considerable anger, which may remain latent or unconscious and which revolves around not being able to be the biological father of the child. This may be lessened if the situation is one in which the sperm of the father is mixed with the sperm of the donor and in which there is at least the possibility that the sperm that does fertilize the ovum is that of the father rather than that of the donor. But there is considerable potential for jealousy; it is frequently the fantasy of being replaced and displaced by this unknown man. These concerns may be dealt with in various ways by various men and are not always disruptive; they can be resolved but must be considered as part of the potential stress of this experience.

The pregnancy itself is, in a way, a relief. Since there is some uncertainty as to whether pregnancy will occur, there is relief and pleasure when a normal pregnancy does develop. Both husband and wife feel pleased. With this pregnancy, there are the usual concerns as well as those unique to the AID pregnancy.

Even a desired pregnancy results in some ambivalence. If this is a first pregnancy, there exist the maturational issues evoked during the pregnancy—the assumption of responsibility for the care of another human being, the transition from being unfettered to being tied to another creature, the worries about being able to be a good parent, the worries about what will happen to one's life or to the relationship between husband and wife—namely, all of the normal concerns of pregnancy. Added to these are somewhat accentuated fears of having a deformed

or defective child, partly due to the donor being unknown, partly due to the feeling of "unnaturalness" about the process. These
concerns may not be central, particularly if the individual has
had one pregnancy before, but if an earlier pregnancy had been
complicated, for instance by an Rh factor or a genetic abnormality, there may be a lot of worry about what is going on this time
and a lot of very subtle comparison with the pregnancy that resulted in a defective baby. As the pregnancy progresses and
seems to be going normally, more positive feelings surface. It
does provide the couple with the possibility of both participating
in a pregnancy that is the same in some ways as if the father were
the biological father. They are both able to have the pleasure of
watching the changes, becoming aware of the fetal heartbeat,
the fetal movements, watching the increase in size, anticipating
the birth of the infant, and preparing for it both externally and
psychologically.

There are a number of different ways in which couples handle telling their family and friends about this. Some are very
open, anticipate the anxiety and criticism, and try to lay it to rest
by explaining about the artificial insemination. Most are much
more secretive, and although they may tell some of their close
friends are unlikely to want it to be generally known.

If the couple does not tell the family and friends, they may
feel isolated. The usual solution for coping with anxieties during
pregnancy and delivery is to derive support from talking, re-
hearsing, and sharing details with friends or family. If this
source of support is not available, where will support come
from? Some find one good friend to talk with, but for others it
may have to come from each other; the situation may be suffi-
ciently stressful that this mutual support may not be readily
forthcoming. It has been the experience of many patients that
their physicians are really not available for this role. Some clinics
that specialize in artificial insemination have sensitive nurses or
other clinicians who are prepared and knowledgeable. Others
do not, and the woman is often left to deal with it alone with
uncertain support from her husband, who may need some help
himself in dealing with his feelings.

There is also a problem about what to tell the child later on.

The wish to be honest with the child may lead to a dilemma. One wants to tell the child the truth. But it may be information that he or she really does not quite know how to handle either because the child is too young or because it is told in a complicated way. One has to assess the stage of cognitive development of the child and decide whether the child is likely to understand the information that is given. It is also important to assess the child's relationship to the parents, his/her self confidence, and his/her feelings about the parents' relationship. Sometimes a child who is trying to understand this feels peculiar and different from other children because insemination is a much less common procedure than adoption, and he/she is not likely to have heard about it. Even adopted children often have many unresolved questions about their biological parents or wonder why their biological parents chose to or had to give them up. They understand even less about artificial insemination. Children usually don't understand exactly what it means until they've at least understood clearly the facts of sexual intercourse and conception, labor, birth and delivery, and it is often not particularly helpful to explain this until they're old enough to be able to place it within the context of a realistic understanding of reproduction.

There are some special situations that occur at an early stage in the postpartum period. Both parents have a great deal of curiosity and interest in the appearance of this baby. The first appearance does not always accurately predict what he or she is going to look like later, but in the postpartum scrutiny of the baby there is more intense curiosity, interest, and anxiety than in an ordinary birth. One looks to see if one can detect characteristics that seem familiar or that seem alien. The couple is often reassured when the baby really looks like the father, even though it is not his biological child, and both parents may find it particularly reassuring that the child will really fit into the family. There is also concern on the part of both the mother and the father about whether the parents will be able to love this child, particularly whether the husband will be able to feel for this child as if it were his own. If there is another child that is biologically his, they worry about whether there will be a difference in the father's feelings toward one child and the other. The first days or weeks postpartum and for some time afterwards may be a kind of testing out of some issues that may make for a good deal of tension.

A positive reaction on the part of the husband can be immensely reassuring to the mother. It is sometimes very difficult to discuss these issues openly because they confront the man with his vulnerability, in terms of his infertility or his contribution to the genetic problem. Here, too, one might say that a certain amount of strong sensitivity is normal. As was mentioned earlier, some couples discuss this more openly than others as a way of handling their concerns. They anticipate questions or doubts and take matters into their own hands. Others tend to keep the issue very much hidden. The form of adaptation to this issue is generally related to the style that a given person or couple uses to deal with other matters as well. If a couple has told family and friends about the artificial insemination, then the issue has already left their control, and the decision about what to tell the child and when to tell the child may not be totally within their control either. They may have to cope with unexpected information as it comes up.

Once the baby is born and is integrated into the family, many of the initial anxieties do subside, particularly as both parents develop a real relationship to this baby as a particular individual. Sometimes, however, fantasies persist, or some of the latent feelings persist and can flare up when precipitated by some other apparently unrelated stimulus such as a threat to the father's masculinity, or some sort of challenge to the control of either or both parents. The father may be relieved to have the problem of his fertility bypassed by having the pregnancy, with some assurance that it is normal. This relief may also be expressed in a positive reaction to and relationship with the child. As in many important situations it is possible for both sets of feelings to be present simultaneously.

It is important to emphasize the very crucial role that support from a sensitive environment and the availability of helpful people can play in how the procedure is experienced by the parents and, in turn, how this affects the way the baby is regarded. This does not mean that a stressful time leads to problems in the relationship with the baby, but it contributes immensely to the difficulties the parents have to surmount. The fact that so many do choose AID and have felt positively about it indicates the importance for many people of having a child.

REFERENCE

David, A., & Avidon, D. Artificial insemination donor: Clinical and psychological aspects. *Fertility and Sterility, 29* (5): 528 – 532. May 1976.

Part IV

DES EXPOSURE
IN UTERO

Chapter 15

INFERTILITY RELATED TO
EXPOSURE TO DES *IN UTERO*
Reproductive Problems
In The Female

Merle J. Berger
Donald P. Goldstein

An association between the use of diethylstilbestrol (DES) and reproductive problems is relatively new to any discussion of the medical aspects of infertility. No infertility discussion can be considered complete without a thorough discussion of this topic: first because a large number of women currently of reproductive age were exposed *in utero;* and second because of the rather disturbing reports that have emerged regarding a high incidence of anatomic abnormalities and reproductive failure in these women.

The purpose of this chapter is to place in proper perspective the ironic DES story from its early use in the prevention of pregnancy wastage to the current implications of its role in causing the same problem. In order to accomplish this and tell a coherent story we will draw on our own clinical experience and describe that of other investigators. After a brief review of the history of the role of DES in reproduction, we shall describe the fertility problems reported in DES exposed females. The implications of these findings including fetal wastage, increased number of therapeutic procedures during pregnancy, and the emotional problems that have resulted from these conditions will be discussed as well. Finally, some mention will be made of the possible treatment for these disorders.

HISTORICAL PERSPECTIVES

The important milestones that led up to our current awareness of reproductive problems of DES exposed women are summarized in Table 1.

DES, a synthetic nonsteroidal estrogen developed in 1931, was first used in 1945 as a medication designed to improve the prognosis in pregnancies complicated by diabetes, toxemia, and prematurity, and to prevent habitual abortion.[1] Subsequently, the indications were extended to include a variety of pregnancy problems thought to be due to placental deficiency of estrogen and progesterone. Despite the fact that a prospective double blind study carried out by Dieckman in 1953 failed to substantiate the beneficial effect of DES, its use continued until recently.[2]

The drug was utilized continually for a quarter of a century before Herbst et al in 1971 described an association with clear-cell carcinoma of the vagina.[3] It is estimated that five million mothers, daughters, and sons were exposed during this period. Amazingly, DES is still approved as a post-coital contraceptive and as a cervical mucus-enhancing agent in infertile women.

The relationship between DES exposure *in utero* and the otherwise rare occurrence of clear-cell vaginal adenocarcinoma was soon confirmed by others. Following shortly thereafter was the demonstration of an association between DES exposure and bizarre gross and microscopic cervico-vaginal abnormalities including adenosis, vaginal stenosis and septa, cockscomb deformity of the anterior cervical lip, and the so called cervical pseudo-polyp deformity (Figure 1).[4] Although it was originally feared that these changes were precursors of clear-cell carcinoma, this relationship has not been demonstrated. It is now apparent that the risk of developing clear-cell carcinoma is quite low and seems to decrease after age nineteen. However, the benign abnormali-

Table 15.1 *Des Exposure*

1931	Synthetic non-steroidal estrogen developed in England
1945	First used clinically in pregnancy (Smith and Smith)
1953	Therapeutic value questioned (Dieckman)
1971	Clear cell CA (Herbst)
1973	Vaginal adenosis/malformations of cervix and vagina (Herbst)
1975	Cervical and vaginal dysplasia (Stafl)
1977	Uterine malformations (Kaufman)
1977	Incompetent cervix (Goldstein)
1979	Reproductive losses (Berger and Goldstein)

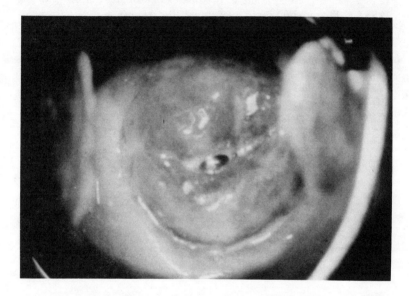

Figure 15-1.
Typical colposcopic cervical and vaginal abnormalities including cockscomb of anterior lip (a), hood (b), and pseudopolyp or ectropian (b). Adenosis is microscopic.

ties are present in up to 90 percent of patients, depending on drug dosage, time initiated, and length of exposure during pregnancy. Stafl and Richart have postulated that women with vaginal and cervical adenosis may ultimately be at increased risk of developing squamous cell cancer as a result of dysplastic changes.[5]

In 1977 a report by Kaufman and co-workers strongly suggested that fertility problems that would have far greater implications than originally anticipated by even the DES cancer association would eventually emerge in exposed women.[6] These problems were presumably due to their findings of bizarre radiologic changes in the uterus, which gave the appearance of an irregular, hypoplastic, and possibly inadequate cavity (Figure 2). Interestingly, the external appearance of the uterine fundus and tubes do not appear to be abnormal. Women who demonstrated the gross cervico-vaginal changes described above demonstrated a greater tendency toward abnormalities on hysterosalpingogram than those with normal appearing cervices. A second study by Haney et al utilizing detailed hysterosalpingographic measurements showed that the endometrial cavity area, upper uterine segment, and endocervical canal width were significantly smaller than normal in the DES exposed patients.[7]

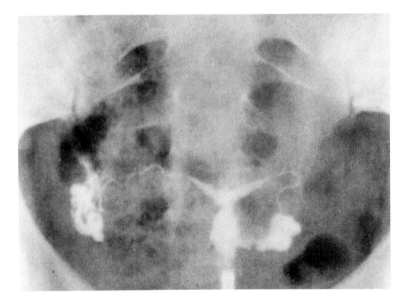

Figure 15-2.
Hysterosalpingogram of "T"-shaped uterus
(no comparison with normal)

Summary of Current Data on Reproductive Performance in DES Exposed Women

In their original report Kaufman's group clearly suspected that there would be problems. This was supported by their initial observation in a few patients that an abnormal hystero-salpingographic uterine configuration correlated with a poor reproductive outcome. Since then other reports and anecdotal cases have hinted at an increased incidence of infertility and fetal wastage.

Our clinical study was based on 69 DES exposed women of whom 55 were actually trying for pregnancy.[8] The remaining 14 patients were not attempting conception but were still "at risk" for pregnancy in that they were not using contraception. Those in the latter group who did conceive eventually chose abortion. Only 46 of the 69 patients were able to conceive, yielding at 66.7 percent conception rate. Clearly, this figure is lower than the 85 percent fertility rate generally quoted in the literature of the normal population. However, the difference is not that great and may be accounted for simply by the high number of infertility patients in our private practices. Hence, the observation that DES exposed women are more likely to be infertile is not established with certainty although there is a strong suggestion that this may be the case.

The reproductive outcome of 32 patients who did conceive and who were desirous of pregnancy sheds some light on the potential problems. Forty-eight percent of the pregnancies that resulted ended in either first or second trimester spontaneous abortion. There were no consistencies in the pattern of this unusually high number of losses. Several very early losses were noted, which included blighted ovum which could have been unrelated to uterine abnormalities. The unusual number of second trimester losses we noted is consistent with the observation that other uterine disorders such as submucus myomas and fusion defects (double uterus) often cause losses in the second trimester in a similar fashion.

Five percent of the pregnancies in our group ended in tubal pregnancy. This is not only a higher incidence than observed in the general population, but also other investigators have noted this as well in DES exposed patients. The mechanism by which this might occur is not clear, so one can speculate a bit. Tubal development is from the embryologic mullerian system, as are the other DES effected structures such as the uterine fundus, cervix, and upper vagina. Although to date no gross abnormalities of the tube have been described, it is reasonable to suggest some as yet undescribed malfunction of tubal motility. Our thinking at the moment is that the uterine cavity is probably more attenuated than hysterographic visualization would suggest, since much of what is seen on x ray and interpreted to be uterine horns may, in fact, represent the interstitial portion of the tube, which seems large only in comparison with the attenuated endometrial cavity. Admittedly, these speculations have little supportive evidence and are meant to be provocative.

Thirteen percent of the pregnancies in our group terminated in third trimester premature deliveries, and three of these infants died. Thirty-four percent of the pregnancies delivered at term and survived. The overall pregnancy success rate was therefore 41.9 percent. All pregnancy success occurred in 16 of 32 patients (50 percent). This means that one half of the patients who were able to conceive were unable to produce a live offspring and that many of those who were able to produce a living child had to undergo several pregnancy losses at all stages of pregnancy in order to eventually succeed.

In a previous publication[9] one of us (DPG) reported eight cases of incompetent cervix in DES exposed patients. All eight of these pregnancies underwent circlage and all ended in a live birth. However, there is some question as to whether this entity is uniformally observed since there is some evidence to the contrary. An additional patient in our study was shown to have a closed cervix just a few days before each of her two midtrimester losses. In addition, many of the hysterosalpingograms in this and other studies seem to show rather long and narrow cervical canals rather than dilated ones.[7] The resolution of this controversy will have to await further studies. It is not clear whether there are going to be an increased number of abnormal presentations in labor due to these uterine deformities. This was not the case in our study but, once again, the numbers are too small for accurate evaluation.

In turning our attention away from the uterine fundal defects for a moment, one would expect to find serious cervical mucus problems as a result of the gross cervical changes noted in these patients. Our observation is that this is not the case. There does not seem to be any deficiency of mucus or mucus secreting cells. As a matter of fact, the pseudopolyp deformity which is often a prominent feature, is composed of mucus-secreting and normal endocervical epithelium. This correlates very well with the abundant mucus noted on examination in the preovulatory phase and by our observation that the post-coital tests have not been abnormal.

There is one bit of contradictory information that suggests the infertility problem may not be as severe as we have indicated. The preliminary data from the DESAD (DES Adenosis) project on fertility in women with DES exposure does show an increased fetal wastage but not a statistically significant one.[10] We feel that this important difference represents a difference in populations in that these investigators reported all patients with a history of DES exposure, and we reported only patients with demonstrable cervical and vaginal abnormalities, which presumably would represent those who tended to be exposed to more DES and at an earlier stage in the pregnancy of the mother.

Oligomenorrhea (infrequent menstruation) is an unrelated but common complaint among many of our DES exposed patients and will clearly complicate any structurally related infertility problems. We have noted this to be associated with clinical signs of androgen excess (hirsutism and acne) more commonly than would be expected in our practices in general. This has been observed by some but not all authors who have looked at this problem.[11] We do not think it is terribly farfetched to propose that like androgen, DES may have a profound effect on hypothalamic regulation and "setting" in the developing fetus. One would expect this effect, if it exists, to be related to dosage and time of exposure as well, which might account for the discrepancies found by different investigators.

Lastly we would like to propose that there may be many

perhaps isolated and unrelated infertility problems due to the anatomical changes observed that will be reported in the ensuing years. We have observed a series of bizarre problems in DES exposed women that would be unlikely to have occurred spontaneously. For instance, two teenagers were noted to have primary amenorrhea, endometriosis, and pelvic inflammatory disease all thought to stem from cervical stenosis. Several patients were erroneously thought to have a double uterus because two cervices were seen on speculum examination when the second cervix was actually a blind false passage made up solely of vaginal folds. A few patients were found to have a conical vagina, which led to either dyspareunia (pain on intercourse) and/or partial occlusion of the cervix. We expect that more will come to light as physicians become more attuned to these disturbing problems.

MANAGEMENT OF INFERTILE DES EXPOSED WOMEN

At the present time the only way to diagnose the presence of a structurally abnormal uterine fundus is via hysterosalpingogram. Although we cannot justify ordering this expensive, sometimes painful, and radiologic procedure on all DES exposed women, we strongly suggest that it be performed on those women who have already demonstrated reproductive problems. Standard techniques can be utilized, but one should take efforts to ensure that the fundus is seen in the true AP diameter in order to properly view the configuration of the uterus. The obstetrician/gynecologist should keep in mind that those women who demonstrate DES related cervical or vaginal abnormalities are more likely to demonstrate uterine abnormalities.

It should be emphasized that at the moment there are no acceptable methods of treatment for the uterine fundal defects described in this paper. In desperation the idea occurred to us that we might try and "stretch" these inadequate fundi by performing a D&C followed by IUD insertion in the hopes of mimicking the beneficial effect occasionally noted from repetitive pregnancies. About a dozen or so patients were treated with mixed results. Although several patients conceived who had been unable to do so, none carried to viability, and post-treatment hysterosalpingograms performed in three patients were not significantly changed in gross appearance.

Clearly, more extensive surgery has no place in the management of these patients. We have had the opportunity to observe several patients who underwent metroplastic (uterine reunification procedures) operations in the mistaken belief that these were bicornuate, septate, or other uterine fusion defects. The results were uniformly disastrous, with permanent infertility due to obliteration rather than enhancement of the uterine cavities postoperatively. Perhaps the use of hysteroscopic surgery may be possible in the future.

The main therapeutic modality that can be utilized successfully in DES exposed women is cervical circlage. As mentioned, patients with small, hypoplastic cervices appear to have a higher incidence of cervical incompetency. These women should be watched carefully during pregnancy from about eight weeks from the last menstrual period and when effacement and/or dilatation is noted, a circlage procedure should be performed. It is not clear to what extent this entity will prove to be a problem; this makes individualization of treatment important.

EMOTIONAL ASPECTS OF INFERTILITY IN DES EXPOSED WOMEN

The emotional impact of the reproductive problems herein described on both the patients and their mothers have been enormous. Anger is probably the most profound and prevalent emotion we have observed. It is unclear to whom this is meant to be directed, but it is often directed toward the physician and certainly the patient/physician relationship can be impaired as a result. Perhaps in attempts to resolve these feelings the patients have often organized or joined groups whose functions are DES related. Naturally these patients additionally share all the emotional difficulties observed in other infertility patients; these are described in detail elsewhere in this book.

The mother's guilt in having taken a medication that caused harm to her offspring is profound and is clearly observed in many ways; most often and most simply by her frequent and inappropriate presence at her mature daughter's visit with the gynecologist. There is probably not much more that can be said about this observation other than to be aware of it and deal with it in a compassionate way.

CONCLUSIONS

The spectrum of a large number of infertility problems due to anatomic and functional abnormalities induced by DES exposure has been a disturbing development during the decade of the 1970s. At the very least it has heightened our awareness of the potentially dangerous side effects of administering medication to pregnant women. Much to the credit of the medical profession the malignant potential of this exposure, initially thought to be the major problem, was soon placed in its proper prospective. A clearer picture of the functional problems associated with the benign DES induced changes is emerging. Included among these are the issue of pregnancy wastage and infertility.

Much remains to be learned about both these areas, but now that we have a sense of the scope of the problem larger and more controlled prospective studies can be expected to yield valuable information.

The only redeeming feature of all this seems to be that no more unborn children are being deliberately exposed to this or other hormonal agents now known to be destructive. When this unfortunate population of women pass the childbearing years, this particular problem will no longer exist.

REFERENCES

1. Smith, O.W., Smith, G.V., & Hurwitz, D. Increased excretion of pregnanediol in pregnancy from diethylstilbestrol with special reference to the problem of late pregnancy accidents. *American Journal of Obstetrics and Gynecology 51*:411, 1946.

2. Dieckmann, W.J., Davis, M.E., et al, Does the administration of diethylstilbesterol during pregnancy have therapeutic value? *American Journal of Obstetrics and Gynecology 66*:1062, 1953.

3. Herbst, A.L., Ulfelder, H., Poskanzer, D.C. Adenocarcinoma of the vagina: association of maternal stilbestrol therapy with tumor appearance in young women. *New England Journal of Medicine 284*:878, 1971.

4. Herbst, A.L., Kurman, R.J., & Scully, R.E. Vaginal and cervical abnormalities after exposure to stilbesterol *in utero*. *Obstetrics and Gynecology 40*:287, 1972.

5. Herbst, A. (ed). Intrauterine exposure to diethylstilbesterol in the human. Proceedings of the Symposium of DES, Chicago, American College of Obstetricians & Gynecologists, 1978, pp. 45–52.

6. Kaufman, R.H., Binder, G.L., Gray, P.M., and Adam, E. Upper genital tract changes associated with exposure in utero to diethylstilbestrol. *American Journal of Obstetrics and Gynecology 128*:51, 1977.

7. Haney, A.F., Hammond, C.B., Soules, M.D., & Creasman, W.T. Diethylstilbestrol induced upper genital tract abnormalities. *Fertility and Sterility 31*:142, 1979.

8. Berger, M.J., Goldstein, D.P. Impaired reproductive performance in DES exposed women. *Obstetrics and Gynecology* Vol. 55, No. 1 pp. 25–27, Jan. 1980.

9. Goldstein, D.P. Incompetent cervix in offspring exposed to diethylstilbesterol in utero. *Obstetrics and Gynecology 52*:73s, 1978.

10. Barnes, A.B. The effect of in utero diethylstilbestrol (DES) exposure in fecundity and fertility in women: preliminary findings from the DESAD Project (abtr). *Fertility and Sterility 30*:737, 1978.

11. Bibbo, M., Gill, W.B., et al: Follow-up study of male and female offspring of DES exposed mothers. *Obstetrics and Gynecology 49*:1, 1977.

Chapter 16

INFERTILITY RELATED TO DES
EXPOSURE *IN UTERO*
Reproductive Problems
in the Male

Alan B. Retik
Stuart B. Bauer

Diethylstilbesterol (DES) is a synthetic estrogen that was first manufactured in the 1930s in London and came into wide use in the 1940s as an effective substitute for natural estrogen. As discussed elsewhere, it wasn't until 1971 that Herbst and Scully noted a strong association between clear cell adenocarcinoma of the vagina in seven of eight young women and DES exposure *in utero*. Although the cancer link does not appear to be as strong as initially suggested, the occurrence of vaginal adenosis, which may be premalignant in these same women, is strikingly high.

The indications for use in pregnancy during the 1940s were as follows: threatened abortion, history of abortion, preventing complications such as premature delivery, pre-eclampsia or eclampsia, diabetes mellitus, and as a "morning after" contraceptive pill.

The best information concerning DES effect on males comes from a prospective study conducted at the Lying-In Hospital at the University of Chicago in 1951 and 1952. A double blind study was undertaken to determine the efficacy of DES during pregnancy for the above mentioned reasons. Eight hundred forty mothers received DES while 806 were given placebo drugs. As of April 1977, 392 DES exposed offspring were traced, of which 163 were males. In the placebo group 304 children were traced, which included 168 males.

Striking differences, especially in the genital region, were noted between the two groups. Epididymal cysts were discovered in 22 exposed males, either unilateral or bilateral, while only eight of the 168 control males had a similar finding. Hypotrophic or small testes were noted in 12 exposed males, with an additional five having significant induration (hardening) of the tunica albuginea or testicular covering. Four males had small phalluses, measuring less than 4 cm long in the flaccid state. All together 41 of the 163 exposed males, or 25 percent, had an abnormal finding on physical examination, while only 11, or 6 percent, of the control males had a similar abnormality.

In another study, undescended testes, hypospadias (opening of the urethra on the undersurface of the penis), and urethral meatal stenosis (narrowing of the urethral opening) were noted in a small number of DES exposed males, but statistically significant correlations could not be made.

Cytologic examination of the urine, prostatic secretion, and the epididymal cyst aspirate in nine patients were undertaken, and no evidence of malignant cells were discovered. All serum hormones, FSH, LH, and testosterone fell within a normal range for both DES exposed and control males. The onset of puberty, first ejaculation, intercourse, sexual drive, height, weight, pubic hair distribution, or breast development did not differ in the two groups.

The most striking finding with long range implications was noted in the semen analysis of 39 DES exposed males when compared with 25 males from the control population. Forty-six percent had a clearly pathologic analysis as compared with 12 percent of control. Thirty six percent had normal analysis, while 18 percent had analyses that fell within the doubtful range; this differs considerably from the control group.

Twenty-six percent of DES exposed males had a count below 20 million sperm per ml with normal being about 40 million.

Three patients were azoospermic. Thirty-eight percent had poor motility and excessive numbers of abnormal forms were noted in 22 percent. Total ejaculate volume was 1.5 ml or less in 26 percent, the normal volume being approximately 3 to 5 cc.

From these studies, one can hypothesize that DES crosses the placenta and has an effect on mullerian duct (the embryologic structure which develops into the female reproductive tract) remnants in the male, mainly the appendix testis and the prostatic utricle. DES may interfere with mullerian inhibiting substance, which is secreted by the fetal testis during the first trimester so that normal male development can proceed. Consequently it may be responsible for some of the physical findings noted after puberty. In addition, DES may have a direct effect on the fetal testis and may possibly impair fetal testosterone production and subsequent spermatogenesis. Further studies are needed to actually clarify these points.

Because the numbers are not large, it is difficult at present to establish a significant correlation between the time of onset and dosage of DES exposure to males *in utero* and the development of subsequent abnormalities. It is probable that DES must be given during the first trimester to at least impair total degeneration of mullerian duct structures. It is uncertain at what stage DES has its greatest effect on the developing testis to impair subsequent spermatogenesis. Pooling data from several studies similar to the one conducted by the University of Chicago group may help to clarify this point.

The possible effect of *in utero* DES exposure to males which needs to be carefully evaluated in the future include exactly what is the fertility potential in these men regardless of semen analysis at present and what effect, if any, there is in their offspring. Also, is there a greater risk for the development of carcinoma of the testis, prostate, or mullerian duct remnants in these men, or even of other types of cancer?

To conclude, we must look to the future. How should one manage the male who has been found to have been exposed to DES *in utero?* Yearly physicals after puberty should be performed. Semen analysis in late teens or early adult years should be obtained, and if abnormal, fertility counseling may be beneficial in improving the patient's chances of bearing children. Lastly, evaluation of the prostate both physically and hormonally, looking for cancer, should be carried out in the middle-aged male. Thus, all of the answers are not complete in the DES picture of male exposure.

REFERENCES

Eliasson, R. Analysis of semen. *Progress in infertility,* 2nd Edition, S.J. Behrman & R.W. Kistner, eds. Boston: Little, Brown and Co., pp 691–713, 1975.

Gill, W.B., Schumacher, G.F.B., & Bibbo, M. Structural and functional abnormalities in the sex organs of male offspring of mothers treated with diethylstilbestrol (DES). *Journal of Reproductive Medicine.* *16*:147–153, 1976.

Henderson, B.E., Benton, B., Cosgrove, M., Baptista, J., Aldrich, J., Townsend, D., Hart, W., & Mack, T.M. Urogenital tract abnormalities in sons of women treated with diethylstilbestrol. *Pediatrics,* *58*:505–507, 1976.

McLachlan, J.A., Newbold, R.R., & Bullock, B. Exposed prenatally to diethylstilbestrol. *Science, 190*:991–992, 1975.

Yalom, I.D., Green, R., & Fisk, N. Prenatal exposure to female hormones. Effect on psychosexual development in boys. *Archives of General Psychiatry.* *28*:554–561, 1973.

Chapter 17

EMOTIONAL ASPECTS OF DES EXPOSURE

Roberta J. Apfel
Susan M. Fisher

DES now has been shown to affect fertility in addition to the other potentially devastating psychological and physiological effects discovered during the last decade. We, as psychiatrists, are interested in the emotional impact DES exposure has had on mothers and offspring. This presentation is based upon our experiences with mothers and mature daughters we have interviewed.[1,2]

We first talked with women who learned of their exposure to DES as something that might be carcinogenic, requiring long-term regular and special examinations (e.g., including colposcopy and biopsy). More recently we have talked with DES daughters who are grappling with their own DES related fertility problems. One striking finding is that physicians tend to underestimate the emotional impact of DES exposure. Our overall impression is that the knowledge of the implications of DES exposure is severely traumatic and that as each new problem is uncovered the trauma may be reexperienced. Supportive professional and personal relationships can creatively help resolve the trauma. However, for the problem of infertility there is a

173

particular irony and constant recurrence of turmoil in mother/ daughter and daughter/doctor relationships.

We found that the DES exposure can be dealt with as any major external trauma or disaster that requires management beyond the acute phase of shock and disbelief. In general there is a period of mourning that has to be experienced. We also found that the mother's and daughter's resolution of the shock and grief depended on two factors: 1) the nature of the conflicts in the woman's life; (i.e. where she was developmentally), and 2) the quality of the physician/patient relationship. We found that when medical personnel treated the woman in a mature, collaborative way, the potential for regression was minimized. The woman felt more responsible, in control, was better able to cope with the experience satisfactorily, and was able to continue her personal growth.

Most women require time to absorb the facts and to discuss the known and unknown. They need to be assured of the ongoing availability of the physician for following through on any problems resulting from DES exposure. We have seen many poignant examples of women who felt betrayed, angered, and disappointed, ironically, not by the DES prescription itself but by the flippant way in which they were told of the exposure and the fact that the impact of the exposure was minimized. The physician who discovers on examination something to indicate the likelihood of DES exposure (adenosis, pseudopolyps, ridging) must go on to explain more, to answer questions, and to deal with some of the ensuing confusion and anxiety. Too often reassurance is given that is false and unconvincing, or technical words are used that frighten and obscure the facts, e.g., erosion. Careful explanation and respectful discussion can allow the mastery of the situation required for the patient to cooperate optimally in the long-term care she will need. The gynecologist becomes an even more crucial person for the DES exposed woman because of the consequence of infertility. In this relationship it is easy to recapitulate the attitude that prevailed when DES was given to the mother. It is especially important for the physician to set a more colleagial tone in the doctor/patient relationship.

One woman stated the complexity of her relationship with her doctor and the feelings of confusion very well:

I said "Wow," a female doctor should really understand how we feel. And I went in. Oh, also I had seen my regular gynecologist the week before for my regular check-up. I went in and I just sit there on the table and she didn't say anything to me, and I just got ready to have the examination. And she starts to examine me. And she says to me "Who cauterized you? Why did you let anybody cauterize you? Like yelling at me for having that treatment done. And I was like, well, "I've been seeing this doctor and that is what he does." And she continues to examine me and says, "Do you know you have an enormous cyst? It is gigantic." And I am sitting there thinking to myself, "Oh my God, I have an enormous, gigantic cyst. My doctor that I can trust, supposedly, examined me a week ago. He didn't even notice this enormous cyst." Like, I am starting to feel crazy. I really felt like the rug had been pulled up from under me. Like, I had been working with somebody I thought I trusted, taking the best care of myself that I possibly could, and here she is, yelling at me and telling me that she found something he didn't the week before and it was enormous. Then she proceeds to tell me that she can't biopsy it now because of the cauterization. And so she says the word biopsy and that says to me "Oh my God, she wants to do a biopsy. That means she is looking to see if it is malignant? She thinks I have an enormous malignancy, a cyst? And I said to her, "Well, is this something you think is serious?" "Well, we don't know until we biopsy it." So I say, "When can you biopsy it?" "Oh, not for at least a month." So it is like I have to sit there for the next month wondering about this enormous cyst she found. Using words like biopsy to patients that have DES who are concerned about having vaginal cancer is really, I mean, something pretty emotionally earth shattering. It was for me anyway." And I called up my old GYN and said, "Hey, I saw this doctor and she said I have this enormous cyst and you just saw me last week." . . . He examined me and said, "Oh yes, I see what she is talking about. It is not enormous and gigantic. It is only this big." He said, "It is nothing to worry about. It is not important."

The resource of support groups for mothers and daughters is essential. Just as RESOLVE, Inc. has met a need and served a purpose in providing self-help, mastery, and decreasing isolation for infertile couples, so the DES Action Project groups have served the DES mothers and daughters. This project communicates with thousands of concerned women, runs support groups, and publishes a newsletter. These groups provide ongoing contact for women of different ages and stages of the problem who can often hear from peers what cannot be understood in the intense interactions with one's own doctor, mother, or daughter. National headquarters for this group are at L.I. Jewish-Hillside Medical Center, New Hyde Park, NY for the East Coast and 1638–B Haight St., San Francisco CA, for the West Coast. Another DES Quarterly (5426 27th St. N.W., Washington, DC) summarizes new medical findings for interested parties. Most reliable information is available from Office of Cancer Communications (DES pamphlets, *not* limited to cancer), National Cancer Institute, Room 10A17, National Institutes of Health, Bethesda, Md. 20014.

Mother/daughter counseling may be a starting point and focus from which other things emerge. It is especially important for the younger, teenaged group of exposed girls to start such discussion—at least informally—in the prepubertal and preadolescent stage. There is a need for early examinations and information because of the malignancy potential especially in the younger age group. It is foolish and destructive to stimulate in a young girl excessive concerns about her future reproductive capability, health, and mortality. The need to judge the right balance and timing in the giving of information is urgently felt by DES mothers. Generally we have recommended an informal arrangement by which mothers take their daughters to their own gynecological examination, gradually introducing them to the experience. Then around puberty, unless there are previous danger signals, regular pelvic examinations can start for the child. The doctor's visits can be an opportunity for mother and daughter to rework some of their anxiety. The young girl, under optimal circumstances, and with no intervening major problem, can grow accustomed to the examinations. The atmosphere of these examinations should be friendly and nonsexual.

Female physicians or nurse practitioners as examiners can make the atmosphere less sexualized but are not automatically by their gender easier for every patient. Men who are aware of the sexual overtones of the exam for a prepubescent girl can do quite well. It is important to be responsive to a mother's anxiety whenever it occurs, to see the daughters when a DES mother calls, and to set up a long-term plan together. The goal is reassurance for the mother and familiarization for the daughter.

The recommendation for male DES exposed offspring is different. While we have not yet had direct experience with this group, we base the following suggestion on knowledge of childhood development and anxieties, and on the possibility that DES male children can be affected by infertility[5] but are currently known to be at greater risk for a life-threatening disease. We think it may be unnecessary to tell a male child at puberty. Sexual functioning of male adolescents at puberty has meaning and significance far beyond the details of spermatogenesis. Since the timing is not so crucial as it is for the girl, we suggest postponing informing the males until late adolescence. The pediatrician or family physician should, of course, be aware earlier of DES exposure so that there will be alertness to any related problems that may require earlier intervention, e.g. malformations. In some families a secret about DES can be more destructive than telling youngsters about the exposure.

Young adult DES daughters may first become painfully aware of the implications of DES exposure when they themselves attempt pregnancy. There is mounting evidence that DES daughters do experience slightly more difficulty in conceiving and substantially more difficulty in carrying a baby to term. In order to produce a normal baby, the average DES daughter will undergo more diagnostic tests and procedures and rely more on medical intervention than someone who has not been exposed.

Young DES exposed women also have concerns about contraceptive choice: the cervical anomalies may make diaphragm fitting undependable and their small uteri may not retain IUDs.

The desire to limit further exposures to hormones has made many DES daughters reject birth control pills. Hormonal contraceptives may add to the DES as a risk factor for tumors later in life; there is no definitive study to date. While the physical effects are uncertain, there are certain emotional effects attached to the taking of drugs similar to those taken by their mothers. The time-bomb effect of DES has made many young women wary of ingesting any drug that might affect their own or their children's reproductive function. Psychologically there is wisdom in the attempt not to repeat past mistakes.

> All the time he (the gynecologist) kept saying, "Don't worry," and he'd explain to me about the effects of DES. There is a lot of fear involved and it was like I just knew that I had something that nobody knew anything about, that there was no 30 year study on. I was the 30 year study and sometimes that was really hard to deal with. Sometimes I have gone though cycles of being really depressed about it. I think the cycles are through. But, it is just very hard always having an unknown."

The DES daughter will be less likely to be reassured by a cavalier paternalistic attitude such as, "Don't worry, it'll be okay" than by a matter-of-fact realistic assessment of the problem, accompanied by appropriate planning. The woman who seems compliant with advice about contraceptive pills may be dealing passively with her concerns and may not take the pills, or may feel resentful at doing so, and may seethe with fear and anger. It is important for gynecologists to take special care to discuss the reasons for advice and/or prescriptions with the DES daughter to optimize her participation in her own treatment and minimize the repetition of the DES trauma her mother experienced and of which she was the unwitting recipient *in utero*. A truly collaborative doctor/patient relationship is the optimal setting in which to anticipate and negotiate any reproductive problems.

The U.S. Department of Health, Education and Welfare *DES Task Force Report*[6] has included in its recommendations programs that meet the psychosocial needs of exposed individuals.

We urge all those who work with DES exposed people to consider the wide-ranging emotional implications of the aftermath of this drug.

REFERENCES

1. Burke, L., Apfel, R.J., Fisher, S., & Shaw, J., Observations on the psychological impact of DES exposure and suggestions on management, *Journal of Reproductive Medicine,* March 1980.

2. Apfel, R.J., & Fisher, S.M. Emotional implications of DES exposure for mothers, daughters, sons and doctors. Presented at the American Psychiatric Association, Chicago, Ill., May 1979.

3. Schwartz, R.W., & Stewart, N.B. Psychological effects of diethyistilbesterol exposure, *Journal of the American Medical Association* 237:252–254, 1977.

4. Shapiro, S., & Slone, D. The effects of exogenous female hormones on the fetus, *American Journal of Epidemiology,* 1979.

5. Gill, W.B., Schumacher, G.F.B., Hubby, M.M., & Blough, R.R. Male genital tract changes in humans following intrauterine exposure to Diethylstilbesterol. Chapter 8. pp 103–119 in Herbst, A.L., & Bern, H.A. *Developmental effects of diethylstilbestrol (DES) in pregnancy* New York: Thieme-Stratton, Inc. 1981.

6. DES Task Force Report, U.S. DHEW, September 1978.

Part V

PRENATAL GENETIC DIAGNOSIS

Chapter 18

MEDICAL ASPECTS OF PRENATAL GENETIC DIAGNOSIS

Wayne A. Miller

Both the infertile couple and the couple at risk for a child with a genetic disorder have a heightened anxiety about conception, the course of a pregnancy, and the outcome of the pregnancy. Neither can approach reproduction as a normal and natural event. In addition, the delay in conception experienced by many infertile couples places them at risk for having a child with a genetic disorder because of advanced maternal age.

Birth defects are a major burden on society and the health care system. It is estimated that only 50 percent of all conceptions result in a live infant. Twenty to 25 percent of all recognized pregnancies terminate during the first 90 days as spontaneous abortions. Of live infants, 4 percent, or 1 in 25, will have a defect present at birth or will develop a genetic disorder during the first year of life. About 50 percent of all perinatal deaths are related to genetic disorders as are 20 to 30 percent of all pediatric hospital admissions. Assessment of the number of years of life lost is a way of appreciating the magnitude of the cost of genetic disorders. The total years of life lost because of genetic disorders is estimated to be four times greater than the total years lost from all forms of heart disease; eight times greater than the total years lost from all types of cancer.

Medical and surgical therapy is applicable in only a few of the more serious types of birth defects. Over the past ten years, tests have been developed that can identify some of the major genetic disorders *in utero*.[1] These provide the parents with the choice of continuing or terminating a pregnancy with an affected fetus. Chromosome abnormalities, open neural tube defects, certain major malformations, certain disorders expressed in fetal blood, and about 100 inborn errors of metabolism can be diagnosed prenatally. The techniques available to diagnose these problems include amniocentesis, ultrasonography, amniography, and fetoscopy.

There are five definite indications and two possible indications for offering prenatal genetic testing. The definite indications identify couples at increased risk for having an offspring with a birth defect that can be identified *in utero*. The possible indications identify couples that need further evaluation to determine whether prenatal testing is applicable.

The definite indications for amniocentesis include. (1) maternal age greater than 35 years, (2) prior birth of a child having a chromosome abnormality, (3) either parent a carrier of a balanced chromosome translocation, (4) at risk for one of the 100 or so inborn errors of metabolism that can be identified *in utero*, and (5) prior birth of an infant with a neural tube defect.

The maternal age-related incidence of chromosome abnormalities increases throughout the reproductive years, but is most marked in the thirties and forties. Most of this increase is due to an increase in the incidence of Down syndrome or Trisomy 21. At maternal age 20, the incidence of Down syndrome is about one per 2,000 births, at age 30, one per 880 births, at age 35, one per 365 births, at age 40, one per 110 births, and at age 45, one per 32 births.[2] The chromosome abnormality associated with advanced maternal age is trisomy, or an extra copy of one chromosome. In Down syndrome, this is an extra copy of a number 21 chromosome, hence the term Trisomy 21 Down Syndrome. This abnormality arises through the process of nondisjunction. In nondisjunction a replicated chromosome fails to separate during cell division so that one daughter cell has an extra copy of the chromosome while the other is missing a copy. Nondisjunction most commonly occurs during the formation of the gametes, a process called meiosis. In normal meiosis there are two cell divisions with only one chromosome replication. This leads to a sperm or egg with 23 chromosomes, one chromosome from each pair. When fertilization occurs, the resultant zygote has a normal diploid chromosome number of 46. If nondisjunction has occurred, one gamete would have 24 chromosomes while the other would have 22 chromosomes. Fertilization with a normal gamete would result in a zygote that had either an extra chromosome, trisomy, or was lacking a chromosome, monosomy. Essentially all autosomal monosomies are lethal, as are most of the autosomal trisomies. Certain of the autosomal trisomies, however, can develop and produce a live infant, but all are associated with serious physical and mental abnormalities.

Empiric studies show that a couple who has had one child with a chromosome abnormality has about a 1 to 2 percent risk of having another child with a chromosome abnormality. This risk is independent of any age-related risk.

A balanced translocation carrier has part of all of one chromosome attached or translocated to another chromosome. Since these individuals have all their chromosome material, there are usually no clinical abnormalities. However, during meiosis these individuals have an increased risk of forming gametes with an abnormal amount of chromosome material. This risk varies from 2 to 20 percent, depending on the type of translocation, which chromosomes are involved, and the sex of the carrier. Quite often translocation carrier parents are identified because of repeated pregnancy losses.

A couple identified by the prior birth of an affected infant or through carrier testing to be at risk for one of the inborn errors of metabolism that can be identified prenatally has a risk of either 25 or 50 percent, depending on the disorder, of having an affected offspring. The best known of these disorders is Tay-Sachs disease.

A couple who has had a child with a neural tube defect such as spina bifida or anencephaly has a risk of about 2 percent of having another affected offspring.

There are two possible indications for prenatal genetic diagnosis, (1) mother is a carrier for an X-linked disorder not directly diagnosable *in utero*, and (2) prior birth of an infant with multiple malformations.

If a woman is a carrier for a serious X-linked disorder, there is a 50 percent risk that any male offspring will have the disease and essentially no risk that female offspring will have the disease (although 50 percent of the female offspring will also be carriers). If prenatal testing for the disorder is not available, these mothers may elect amniocentesis to identify the sex of the fetus by chromosome analysis. Since 50 percent of the males and none of the females will be affected, the woman may choose to continue only the female pregnancies.

A couple with the prior birth of a child with multiple malformations should be evaluated to determine the cause of the anomaly. If the cause is genetic and the couple is at risk for a recurrence then it should be determined if the defect can be identified by amniocentesis testing or through one of the visualization procedures such as ultrasound, amniography, or fetoscopy.

Amniocentesis is a simple technique. We recommend strongly that ultrasound examination be performed prior to or concurrently with the amniocentesis. Ultrasound examination identifies the gestational age, location of the placenta, presence of a multiple gestation, and gross abnormalities of the fetus. Menstrual dating or pelvic examination of uterine size can be inaccurate, while ultrasound measurement of the biparietal diameter of the fetal skull should be accurate to within one week of the true gestational age. Proper assessment of gestational age is crucial to timing of the amniocentesis and interpretation of certain results. Prior to 14 weeks of gestation there is little amniotic fluid and amniocentesis is difficult and more dangerous to the fetus than at a later gestational age.

The test for neural tube defects is a measurement of the amount of alpha-fetoprotein in the fluid. The normal values for this chemical are high at 14 weeks gestation and decrease as gestation progresses. A measured value interpreted as abnormally high for 18 weeks gestation could be normal if the gestational age was truly 14 weeks.

Placental localization allows for identification of the safest area for needle insertion. Placental trauma is the most common cause of fetal loss associated with amniocentesis. Localization of the placenta by ultrasound allows the physician to avoid puncture of the placenta or at least the area of insertion of the cord. The presence of a multiple gestation with separate amniotic sacs requires amniocentesis of each sac in order to accurately assess the status of each fetus. Ultrasound can identify such pregnancies and can help guide needle insertion into each sac. Major malformations such as anencephaly and omphalocoele can be detected by ultrasound examination. Experimental studies show that ultrasound can be useful in identifying fetal kidney, heart, or limb malformations.

Amniocentesis can be performed between 14 to 20 weeks of gestation. We believe the optimal time is 16 to 17 weeks of gestation. At this stage there is a relatively large fluid volume (in comparison to 14 weeks) yet there is sufficient time to complete the tests. The procedure is straightforward. With the woman in the supine position the abdomen is prepped and draped and the needle inserted at the predetermined area. Fifteen to 25 ml of fluid is removed and transported to the laboratory, and the fluid is centrifuged to separate the cells from the supernatant (fluid). The cells have been shed by the skin, lungs, kidneys, and amnion of the fetus. The cells are grown in culture and stained to allow for chromosome analysis or processed for biochemical studies. The fluid is analyzed for the amount of alpha-fetoprotein.

A study conducted by the National Institute of Child Health and Human Development showed no increase in the rate of fetal loss in women who had amniocentesis in comparison with women who did not.[3] This study has been interpreted as indicating that there is little or no risk to the procedure. More recent studies have shown a very definite risk to the fetus. I feel that this risk of miscarriage is not clearly defined, but is probably in the range of 1 per 100 to 1 per 300 procedures. The accuracy of the testing was greater than 99 percent in the NICHD study. Most of the errors in diagnosis occurred because maternal cells were obtained during the amniocentesis and these established in culture rather than fetal cells. This is now guarded against by use of a needle with a stylet for the procedure, flushing of the needle by withdrawing a few ml of fluid and discarding it before obtaining the fluid for the test, and by establishment of separate cultures for each sample in the laboratory. Another cause of erroneous diagnosis was due to human error, either sample mix-up or misinterpretation of the chromosome results. The third area of incorrect diagnosis was in interpretation of the alpha-fetoprotein measurements. The availability of techniques such as acetyl cholinesterase isozyme assay, ultrasound, and amniography have now made it possible to confirm the alpha-fetoprotein findings.

The NICHD study also defined the failure rate for amniocentesis, both in terms of inability to obtain fluid and failure of cells to establish in culture. This study showed a 6 percent failure to obtain fluid and a 9 percent culture failure. I believe that these rates of failure are unacceptable. The maximum rate of failure for either category should be 1 to 2 percent.

The current feeling of society is that pregnancy and the birthing process should return to its natural state. I strongly agree with this, but feel that we can maintain the standard of care that has evolved from our technological advances while re-establishing the humanity in obstetrical care. Pregnancy and birth is a natural process, but problems do occur. It is medicine's role to offer a couple the greatest chance of having healthy, viable offspring. In regard to prenatal genetic diagnosis, except in the case of a woman over 35, our ability to do so generally occurs only after the birth of an affected infant.

As an example, 90 to 95 percent of all neural tube defect infants are born to couples with no previous history of genetic problems. Once a couple has had a child with this problem, we know that they have a risk of about 2 percent that this will occur again, and they should be offered prenatal genetic testing. But we have not been able to identify the 1 in 500 couples without any prior history that will have a child with this problem. Recent studies have shown that neural tube defects are associated with an elevation of alpha-fetoprotein in the mother's blood. This may provide us with a safe, inexpensive way of screening the entire population of pregnant women for neural tube defects. Results from the British study on this screening process indicate that this technique could identify 84 percent of all fetuses with an open neural tube defect.[4] Since it is a screening process, about 5 percent of all women tested will have an abnormal test and will be selected for further testing. About one third of these will eventually have amniocentesis, and 1 in 12 of these will have an abnormal fetus. Critics of this program say that this procedure evokes undue concern in the women who are not in a high risk group for birth defects that are initially identified as "abnormal" and then found to be normal. This is a valid complaint and needs to be addressed prior to widespread application of this procedure.

REFERENCES

1. Miller, W.A., & Erbe, R.W. Prenatal diagnosis of genetic disorders. *Southern Medical Journal 71*:201, 1978.

2. Hook, E.B., & Hamerton, J.L. The frequency of chromosome abnormalities detected in consecutive newborn studies—differences between studies—results by sex and by severity of phenotypic involvement. *Population cytogenetics,* E.B. Hook and I.H. Porter, eds. New York: Academic Press, 1977, pp. 63–80.

3. NICHD National Registry for Amniocentesis Study Group. Midtrimester amniocentesis for prenatal diagnosis: Safety and accuracy. *Journal of the American Medical Association 236*:1471, 1976.

4. U.K. Collaborative Study on Alpha-fetoprotein in Relation to Neural-tube Defects. Maternal serum-alpha-fetoprotein measurement in antenatal screening for anencephaly and spina bifida in early pregnancy. *Lancet 1*:1323, 1977.

5. Fuchs, F. Genetic Amniocentesis. *Scientific American,* Vol. 242, No. 6, p. 47–53, June, 1980.

Chapter 19

THE ROLE OF THE GENETIC COUNSELOR

Stacey Tsairis Kacoyanis

This presentation will describe our approach to the amniocentesis patient at the Prenatal Laboratory of the Massachusetts General Hospital. A description of the counseling process and situations that present special problems in counseling will be discussed, followed by a summary of three studies describing patient responses to prenatal genetic studies.

It is of utmost importance that a woman undergoing amniocentesis be given an in-depth explanation about the entire testing process. The following information should be included in the presentation: the reasons for performing the testing, the benefits and limitations of the testing, the risks involved in amniocentesis, the accuracy of the testing, and a description of the testing to include the procedure itself, the laboratory process, the length of time required to complete the testing, and the methods of reporting the test results. This information is given to every woman referred to our facility for amniocentesis and is presented preferably to both the patient and her husband in an informal, private discussion. This usually encourages the couple to express their concerns about the testing, concerns acknowledged and discussed by the counselor. Many misconceptions surface at this time and can be corrected before developing into unnecessary sources of anxiety. A written pamphlet containing basic information is distributed to each patient. Also, continued contact is encouraged by providing our phone number, and questions are welcomed regarding the progress of their testing. The time invested in such discussions with the patient or couple is substantial, usually a minimum of 30 minutes. It is felt that the investment is a worthwhile one, for the following reasons:

First and foremost, the discussion is important for the patient. She is given sufficient information to understand the testing process and thus will be able to make decisions regarding the management and outcome of her pregnancy. By providing accurate facts and by addressing some patient concerns, it is hoped that the patient's anxiety can be somewhat reduced. Availability of our staff by telephone provides a continual source of information and emotional support that is absolutely essential to assist the patient through the long waiting period fraught with the fear of the as yet unknown outcome of the tests. If unexpected test results arise, the initial counseling sessions have already given the patient the basic information that lays the groundwork for the understanding of the potential problem at hand. The information obtained by our amniocentesis patients will be shared with their friends. Since amniocentesis has not yet become a "household word" this process will assist the educational efforts already underway to make women aware of the availability of amniocentesis. The benefit of these discussions is that they make the Prenatal Laboratory staff aware of the concerns of each patient. There is much to learn from their experiences with prenatal genetic diagnosis so that our services can be improved. Follow-up studies on our patient population are planned to survey their attitudes and reactions to prenatal genetic studies.

As a preview to the discussions of some of the problems encountered in prenatal genetic diagnosis, a description of our patient population and information emphasized in counseling is necessary. The majority of patients have already had amniocentesis performed by their obstetricians when they arrive at our facility. They deliver their amniotic fluid sample for testing in our laboratory, and it is at this time that the relevant information previously described is discussed. An increasing number of patients are being referred to our facility for amniocentesis itself, which includes ultrasonography performed prior to the tap. After initial phone contact with the patient, the written pamphlet describing the testing is sent to her prior to her appointment. Ample time is then set aside for a discussion of the testing before the amniocentesis. In either case, approximately 88 percent of our patients have been referred because of advanced maternal age.

Certain information is emphasized in our discussions with patients because they are often not aware of some of the following facts. The first is the limitations of prenatal testing. All too often this test is described as being able to predict whether or not a baby will be "normal." This leads to the misconception that the testing will detect all birth defects; this is not accurate. We discuss the possibility of failure to establish a successful amniotic cell culture, which would result in the inability to obtain results unless a re-tap is performed. The possibility of obtaining results that may present problems in interpretation is explained. In the course of prenatal genetic diagnosis there are certain situations that can present problems in counseling. Certain cases may require further testing. For example, an elevation of alpha-fetoprotein may result, usually, although not always, requiring repeat amniocentesis. Another example occurs when there is a minor variation in fetal chromosomes; it is usually necessary to obtain blood samples from both parents so that we might examine their chromosomes for the same variant. If the same variant is found, this would not cause concern about the well-being of the fetus. A potential problem exists of discovering a variant that is not traced to one of the parents and has not been previously described in the medical literature. In such cases counseling would be ineffective since it would be impossible to clearly interpret the results. This problem is discussed in the initial counseling session and parents are aware of this potential dilemma. Both of these situations, despite our previous discussions, usually cause the patient great concern, and she frequently develops a pessimistic expectation concerning the outcome of her pregnancy. By providing an accurate and complete description of the further testing to be done, patient anxieties can usually be somewhat reduced. It is also common to find that the patient, because of anxiety, retains little of what was originally explained, and a review of the facts is useful.

In other cases testing may sometimes yield equivocal results; these can occur in either alpha-fetoprotein or chromosomal analysis. When the medical literature does not document previous cases of a similar nature, there is little or no knowledge on which to base a diagnosis. The previously described case of a chromosome variant in the fetus not traceable to parents exemplifies this situation and presents a serious dilemma for both the parents and the counselor. Still other problems arise when the results of prenatal testing yield abnormal results of questionable clinical consequence in the fetus. An example of this situation would be a sex chromosome abnormality such as trisomy X. The karyotype in this case would reveal a female child with chromosome constitution of 47, XXX. The incidence of trisomy X is approximately 0.7 per 1000 females. Genetic counseling is a difficult task when trisomy X is prenatally diagnosed since these individuals do not seem to form a well-defined syndrome. The majority of trisomy X females have normal reproductive function and have only a slightly increased risk of bearing chromosomally abnormal offspring. However, they are often mentally retarded. Other sex chromosome abnormalities that would present difficulties in genetic counseling are Turner's syndrome, a single X chromosome, which occurs in approximately 1 in 2500 females. These females almost always have normal mental function but are infertile. The 47, XXY male or Klinefelter syndrome male occurs in approximately 1 in 1000 males. With this syndrome psychotic tendencies and a slightly lowered IQ are common, and all are infertile. The 47, XYY male has an incidence of approximately 1 in every 1000 males. These men are fertile, and the tendency towards increased criminality has not been clearly documented.

Parents are usually faced with serious dilemmas when these cases are diagnosed prenatally. At best, genetic counseling can present the factual information and provide support to the parents, who then must make a very difficult decision. When the test results indicate a serious abnormality in the fetus, such as Down syndrome or Trisomy 21, the results are conveyed to the referring physician by telephone; he/she then contacts the parents. In most cases the explanation of the problem is handled by the private physician, but the option for additional counseling at our facility is always available. If the patient opts to terminate the pregnancy, a referral can be made for this by our facility at the request of the physician.

While much information is available about the technical aspects of amniocentesis, very little information is available concerning the impact of such studies on participating couples. One such study done at the University of Alabama surveyed 196 patients by means of a short answer questionnaire with 80 percent of the patients responding. When patients were asked what their major concerns were prior to amniocentesis (more than one response was allowed), 66 percent replied that it was whether the test would show an abnormality, 60 percent said that they were concerned about possible injury to the fetus, and 50 percent indicated that the possibility of having to make a decision about abortion was a major concern. Less concern was expressed at the pain involved in the procedure and the risk of miscarriages, both approximately 30 percent. In response to the question, "When you first had amniocentesis did you plan to end the pregnancy if your tests showed you were carrying an abnormal fetus?" 71 percent said yes, 6 percent no, and 23 percent were undecided. The significant proportion of undecided responses points to the fact that prenatal diagnosis should be available to women without any conditions regarding their attitude towards abortion prior to amniocentesis.

Regarding the question: "If you became pregnant again, would you have this test again?" 94 percent indicated that they would, 4 percent said no, and 2 percent were undecided. When asked if they would recommend this test to others, 98 percent said that they would and 2 percent no. The overwhelmingly favorable response indicates that amniocentesis and prenatal genetic diagnosis were generally considered positive and worthwhile experiences.

It is interesting to note that four out of the five respondents who had a therapeutic abortion because of abnormal test results responded favorably to the last two questions. Among those respondents who would not elect to have the test again, one had a fetal death of unknown cause subsequent to amniocentesis, one received no results because of inadequate cell growth, one elected to carry a Trisomy 21 or Down syndrome infant to term, two opposed therapeutic abortion, and one offered no reason. When patients were asked to state ways in which to improve the amniocentesis process, the suggestion most often made was to decrease the waiting time for results.

Another study on the impact of amniocentesis on mothers and infants was conducted at the University of Colorado Medical Center. Twenty-two infants and mothers were assessed at the time of the infants' first birthday. The Bailey Infant Scale of Mental and Motor Development was administered to these children and all were within a normal range. Each mother was personally interviewed 15 months after amniocentesis and had received genetic counseling prior to amniocentesis. Of this group 19 out of 22 considered it as a positive experience. Although anxiety is a difficult and controversial variable to measure, an attempt was made to do so by breaking up the amniocentesis procedure into its various temporal components: first, the anticipation of the test; second, the experience of the actual tap; third, worry while waiting for test results; fourth, worry in the remainder of the pregnancy about the effects the test had on the pregnancy or the infant; and fifth, worry after delivery about possible harm to the infant from the test. All these components were distinguished from the high anxiety caused by the possibility of having a defective child.

Of these five components the waiting period between amniocentesis and final diagnosis contributed most frequently to patients' anxiety. Twelve women were acutely concerned during this time. Of the eight women who were very worried about having a defective child, seven, in fact, had already had a defective child. Ten of the 14 women who had low concern about such a possibility were referred for reasons of advanced maternal age.

These women saw the test as part of their regular prenatal care and were usually following their physician's advice with the inner certainty that their babies would be fine.

At the 1978 meeting of the American Society of Human Genetics, a presentation was made on a recent poll of 250 women in Halifax, Nova Scotia. Eighty-three of these 250 women were over the age of 35, and 167 were controls. When questioned as to whether they would have amniocentesis only 18 percent said yes. Of this group, 47 percent said they would consider therapeutic abortion if some abnormality were found. Twenty-three said they would not consider termination of their pregnancy, and 30 percent were undecided. Twenty-four percent of the women polled were totally unaware of the risks or the availability of the tests. But 100 percent agreed that the tests should be offered.

Although we have not begun to formally survey our approximately 550 amniocentesis patients at the Prenatal Laboratory, this is planned in the future through the use of a short-answer questionnaire. However, a subjective evaluation of our patients' reactions and attitudes towards prenatal genetic diagnosis indicates that they view the experience overall as positive, even in the few instances of an abnormal test result. The overwhelming majority of our patients expressed their gratitude for the information presented at genetic counseling sessions and were usually delighted when our phone number was given to them for further information and support. Many have used this hot line and have claimed that it has helped them through a very long and difficult waiting period.

REFERENCES

Finley, S.C., Varner, P.D., Vinson, P.C., & Finley, W.H. Participants' reaction to amniocentesis and prenatal genetic studies. *Journal of American Medical Association, 238*:2377 – 2379, 1977.

Mueller-Huebach, E., Garver, K.L., & Ciocco, A.M. Prenatal diagnosis of trisomy X: Its implications for genetic counseling. *American Journal of Obstetrics and Gynecology. 127*(2):211 – 212, 1977.

Robinson, J., Tennes, K., & Robinson, A. Amniocentesis: Its impact on mothers and infants. A 1-year follow-up study. *Clinical Genetics.* *8*:97 – 106, 1975.

Sorenson, J., Swazey J., and Scotch N., *Reproductive pasts reproductive futures genetic counseling and its effectiveness.* Monograph of the March of Dimes Birth Defects Foundation, Vol. 17, No. 4, New York: Alan R. Liss Inc., 1981.

Chapter 20

THE AMNIOCENTESIS EXPERIENCE

Ann Edwards Boutelle

For nine years I have been attempting to come to grips with
what amniocentesis has meant to me. Underlying everything, of
course, is my profound gratitude to the researchers, doctors,
technicians, and nurses who have made amniocentesis possible,
and who, in turn, have made my three children possible. Without amniocentesis, Jonathan (born in 1973), Laura (born in
1976), and Alec (born in 1982) would not now exist.

There is a genetic problem in my family. I have a balanced
translocation (45 chromosomes instead of the normal number),
and I am a carrier of Downs syndrome. Knowing this, I would
never become pregnant and carry a child to term unless I could
have amniocentesis.

So there is a debt there, a debt shared by many other wom-
en. Thousands of children have been made possible, children
who otherwise might never have been conceived. Moreover, amniocentesis has helped women to pursue their careers and delay
childbearing. For many thousands of women, it has made the
latter part of pregnancy a joyous and optimistic time.

Yet looking back on my own experience I am aware that all
was not simple and easy. And in talking to other women, I have

discovered that they too found certain aspects of the experience difficult.

Basic information about the procedure and about the risks is often difficult to obtain; this lack of information is responsible for needless stress and anxiety. We need to know when the tap should be performed. We need to know the risk to the fetus, the risk of having an abnormal child. What is it going to feel like? Is there going to be much pain? How will I feel after it's over? What on earth is a B-scan?

The ultrasound part of the experience provides a good example of the benefits of preparation. The various names of the procedure can, to the uninitiated, sound terrifying. Yet, over and over again, women report the pleasurable wonder of it all: "It was fantastic!" "I never knew it was going to be like that: absolutely painless, first of all—and then there was the picture of the fetus on the screen." "It was moving and exciting and wonderful." Husbands and partners should be encouraged to attend. Many women express their regret that the prospective fathers have been excluded because of a basic lack of information: "I wish that I'd known what it would be like. I wish that Sam could have been there to see." "It was the first time I saw my baby. I would have liked him to be there, to share that moment with me."

Patients should be encouraged to ask questions, and should—if necessary—take it upon themselves to find out what will happen before, during, and after the tap. Even the routine, if unexpected, can create undue turmoil. For example, patients are sometimes faced with a long and complicated consent form. This can be intimidating if presented at the time of the tap or just after it. Husbands have been known to refuse to sign, to march up and down the corridors, sending everyone into a needless panic. Adequate preparation would eliminate this extra stress.

Patients should also inquire about the delivery of the fluid to the laboratory. For example, in Massachussetts the patient is expected to deliver her own sample, sometimes to a lab a considerable distance away. One husband who was due to go out on business to the west coast had delayed his departure so that he could be with his wife at the time of the tap. It came as a complete surprise to both that they were suddenly expected to deliver the sample. The husband's plane was due to leave. The wife didn't feel like driving an unknown route on her own. And the fluid sample ended up taking a cab in solitary splendor. Once again, access to the most basic information would have contributed greatly to everyone's peace of mind.

Armed with the basic information the patient can better prepare. It is good if someone can go with her at the time of the tap: husband, partner, or friend. Often, partly because of the psychological strain, she may feel a little shaky after the tap, and support is a great help. If she already has children, it is a good idea to arrange for child care, so that she does not have to rush around picking up toys and cleaning faces if she doesn't feel up to it. If she feels perfectly fine, as many women do, she can always celebrate the success of the tap by going off to see a movie or visit a friend.

It is also useful to know that there is much less pain involved than is often anticipated. I myself am squeamish about needles, and I look resolutely in the other direction whenever blood has to be drawn. In amminocentesis, of course, the needle is especially long, and it is entering an area which, to the patient, seems espcially vulnerable, especially sensitive. It usually doesn't hurt very much. And while this may be a pleasant surprise, it might be even more pleasant to know this before the tap.

Before and during the tap, anxiety is usually focused more on the danger to the fetus than on the possibility of physical pain. This is a legitimate anxiety, and the risk to the fetus should be acknowledged. Only then can it be balanced by the patient and by her advising physician against the anxiety and the risk of having an abnormal child. If the patient selects a qualified and experienced physician to perform the tap she will be able to feel less anxious. Confidence in the physician is, I am sure, a major factor in alleviating anxiety and in reducing guilt. Many of us feel torn about amniocentesis: we don't want to expose what may well be a normal, healthy fetus to the risk yet we shy away from the prospect of an abnormal child. A trustworthy doctor can help us here.

The most trying part of the experience is undoubtedly the period between the tap and the arrival of the results. The waiting period is long—three to five weeks—and it is a rare woman who can breeze her way through this time: "I never even thought about it. I was sure that everything was going to be okay. I felt that it would have been irresponsible *not* to have amniocentesis. But afterwards I just forgot all about it."

For most of us, however, this waiting period is very difficult. The fetus is now moving in noticeable and clear ways. There is a horror about the thought of having to undergo a late abortion. What would it be like? We don't know, yet are appalled at the prospect. It is a nightmare lurking insistently around the corner in these long weeks.

What may appear simple at the beginning of the amniocentesis experience appears more and more complex as the pregnancy progresses. There is guilt even in the contemplation of aborting an abnormal fetus. Some women have sleeping problems; some find it impossible to think of anything else. At the center of everything is the difficulty of accepting the pregnancy in a fully committed way while at the same time considering the possibility of ending it. Even if there is no pressure on the physician's part for the women to decide what she would do if faced with the diagnosis of an abnormal fetus, most women find themselves asking, "What if . . . ?" As one women put it, "I knew that it would have haunted me for the rest of my life. I would have known that there was someone I hadn't allowed to live." Either prospect—abortion or Downs syndrome—is painful to contemplate.

All this, of course, is happening at a time when the pregnancy is becoming increasingly conspicuous to those around you. And this complicates the issue of whom to tell and what to say. There are many possible approaches here; what feels comfortable and natural for one women may be unsuitable for another. For example, "I saw it as a public health and education kind of issue—pro-women's rights, pro-abortion, and so on. And so I told everyone about it. If anyone didn't understand, then I'd explain it to them." Other women tell nobody, nobody at all, apart from the husband—and are then faced with the necessity of disguising (as far as is possible) their pregnant state. Many find some kind of compromise, such as announcing the pregnancy, but staying silent about the amniocentesis. Sometimes there is a problem with the grandparents-to-be. If there is a great desire on their part for grandchildren, then the suggestion that all may not be well can be difficult for them to deal with. Neighbors, colleagues, and bosses all present a challenge.

What do you tell existing children? The answer may depend partly on the child's age. When I was pregnant with Laura, Jonathan was only three years old—and too young in the judgment of my husband and myself to be surrounded by mysterious conversations about tests and waiting periods. Partly for his sake I told very few people about the pregnancy, and this extra consideration added more stress to an already stressful time. When parents are in doubt about what to say, a sensitive pediatrician can often help.

If a woman wants to keep the pregnancy a secret, then there is the very real question of what to wear during this period. Loose-fitting clothes several sizes too large and a collection of silhouette-obscuring jackets will usually work. Maternity clothes announce pregnancy, and few people will dare ask the question until they see that sign. (Incidentally, most amniocentesis-women wait to buy maternity clothes until they receive a favorable verdict. A typical reaction to the good news is to rush out and buy—with pride—the jacket that she can now expect to wear for several months.)

A good verdict brings with it exhilaration and a delighted plunge into full acceptance of the pregnancy. Knowledge of the sex of the fetus often accompanies the results. While some women prefer *not* to know, saving the surpirse of discovery for the delivery-scene, most women request this knowledge. Psychologically it is a wonderful boost after the weeks spent in limbo to know that there is a little girl or a little boy in there growing happily. The family can finally begin to love the son or daughter in anticipation of the birth.

The impact of all this on a women's day-to-day living is extensive. It lasts for several months, a good half of the pregnancy. The impact on the entire family is also very real, and support here is essential. Women are not alone in this experience—although each may feel lonely, freakish, guilty. Support is there: in the love expressed by our own families, in the concern of other families, and in the lives of the women who have gone before us. We need each other. And we can help each other.

REFERENCE

Boutelle, Ann. Suspence in pregnancy. *Vogue*, September, 1978, pp. 307.

Part VI

IN VITRO FERTILIZATION

Chapter 21

IN VITRO FERTILIZATION

Machelle M. Seibel and Melvin L. Taymor

Introduction

The birth of the world's first test-tube baby in 1978 was heralded as a miracle. However, what in fact occurred was not a miracle but the culmination of experience and information gained over the last 25 years by a large number of scientists working in this area. Today over 100 centers are performing in vitro fertilization (IVF) throughout the world. This overview is intended to describe the steps necessary to perform IVF, the present state of the art, and the ethical considerations that must be addressed.

The Normal Process of Fertilization

In order to understand how IVF works, it is necessary to understand how fertilization occurs under normal situations. Each month at midcycle, an oocyte (egg) is ovulated into the fallopian tube. When intercourse occurs several million sperm are deposited into the vagina, and a few dozen of them are able to swim through the uterus and into the fallopian tube. One sperm will penetrate the oocyte and fertilization occurs. The fertilized egg remains in the fallopian tube for about two days and grows to approximately 4 to 8 cells. This is called an embryo. At this time, the embryo enters the uterus where it implants and grows over the next nine months. In IVF the fallopian tubes are bypassed. The oocyte is removed from the ovary immediately prior to ovulation and is placed in a petri dish with sperm from the husband. One sperm will penetrate the oocyte, and fertilization occurs. The fertilized egg remains in the petri dish for about two days and develops into an 4 to 8 cell embryo. At this time the cluster of cells is placed into the uterus where it implants and grows for the next nine months.

INDICATIONS FOR IVF

When IVF was first attempted, its application was limited to women with absent or severely damaged fallopian tubes. Since that time the indications for IVF have been greatly expanded. Couples in which the husband's sperm count is either severely reduced or the sperm are incapable of living in the wife's cervix are now included. Successes have also occurred in patients with severe endometriosis and in cases of unexplained infertility. These indications include most areas of infertility and therefore create great potential application for IVF.

OVULATION TIMING

One of the most important aspects of IVF is to obtain an oocyte immediately prior to ovulation. One of the body's hormones, luteinizing hormone (LH), consistently increases about 36 hours prior to ovulation. For this reason, either blood or urine samples are obtained every three hours in order to determine precisely when the LH rise has occurred. Urine samples are certainly simpler and less painful than blood samples, but blood results are more accurate and more reliable. The blood tests are obtained through a small catheter that remains in an arm vein for several days. Repeated veno-punctures are therefore eliminated. In those few patients who have very difficult veins in which to place a catheter and would therefore require repeated veno-punctures, the urine method may be superior. Daily ultrasound examinations of the pelvis are also performed to observe the growth of the follicle (cyst) that houses the oocyte. The follicle grows to slightly less than one inch in diameter. A laparoscopy for oocyte retrieval is usually scheduled thirty-two to thirty-five hours after onset of the LH rise. There are several difficulties in timing ovulation. The first is that the patient is never quite sure which day is to be "the day." This added stress may actually postpone ovulation for several days, thus making the situation worse. Second, it is difficult for the doctors to schedule the operating room since only thirty-two to thirty-six hours notice is possible. Most busy hospitals book surgery weeks in advance and therefore no operating room time is available. Third, only one oocyte develops in the natural cycle. If more than one oocyte were available, a higher chance of success might be possible.

Some of these problems can be circumvented by using fertility drugs to stimulate ovulation. The injectable type is called human menopausal gonadotropin (hMG) and the oral form is called clomiphene citrate. These drugs are usually begun on day five of the cycle and are administered for five to eight days. Daily pelvic ultrasounds are performed beginning on day 10 of the cycle. When the follicle attains a certain critical size, about $3/4$'s of an inch, the hormone human chorionic gonadotropin (hCG) is injected intramuscularly to trigger ovulation, which will occur about thirty-six hours later. Stimulating ovulation has two distinct advantages. The first is convenience. By giving hCG in the evening, laparoscopy can be performed during regular operating room schedules. The second advantage is that two eggs usually develop, which increases the chances of success. Neither the fertility drugs nor the ultrasound examinations have been shown to be harmful.

LAPAROSCOPIC ASPIRATION

The next step in IVF is to aspirate the oocyte from the follicle. This is done with the aid of a laparoscope. The patient is
usually asleep for this procedure. A small ½ inch incision is
made in the lower curve of the umbilicus. A needle through
which a mixture of gas flows is placed through the incision into
the abdomen. This gas will be removed at the end of the procedure. When the abdomen is filled with gas, the pelvic organs are
easier to see, and the oocyte recovery is simpler. The needle is
then removed and a laparoscope about the size of a long
ballpoint pen is placed through the incision into the abdominal
cavity. A second ½ inch incision is then made in the pubic hair
line. A probe is placed through the incision to hold and stabilize
the ovary. Occasionally a third ½ inch incision is required to
allow a second probe to be inserted. Under direct vision a needle
is placed directly into the follicle and by means of gentle suction
the oocyte and its surrounding fluid are aspirated into a special
collecting device. The contents are placed into a petri dish and,
with the aid of a microscope, the oocyte is identified. In capable
hands oocytes can be recovered 80 to 90 percent of the time.

FERTILIZATION IN VITRO

Fertilization in vitro of human oocytes can now be achieved
in the vast majority of attempts. Several techniques have been
described and subtle details vary from center to center. A generalized description follows.

The patient's husband is asked to produce a semen specimen by masturbation shortly before the scheduled laparoscopy.
The semen, or liquid portion of the ejaculate that surrounds the
sperm, is not sterile and must be separated from the sperm. This
is done by mixing a small aliquot of semen with a sterile culture
medium in a test tube. By centrifuging the mixture the washed
sperm form a pellet in the bottom of the test tube, and the un-
sterile wash can be poured off. The sperm pellet is then resuspended in culture medium, and the entire process is repeated.

The third time the sperm pellet is resuspended, the sperm and culture medium are placed into an incubator for one hour. This washing process produces bacteria-free sperm and also allows for capacitation, the process by which sperm attain the capacity to fertilize an oocyte. In the meantime the oocyte has been retrieved and placed in its own culture media for several hours.

When the proper amount of time has passed, approximately 500,000 to one million sperm are placed into the culture media containing the oocyte. They are allowed to incubate together for approximately eighteen hours. The oocyte is then visualized under a microscope to determine if fertilization has occurred.

The fertilized oocyte is then transferred into a second culture medium which consists in part of a sample of the patient's blood, and is incubated for an additional twenty-two hours. At this time the fertilized egg is ready to be transferred to the uterus.

Most institutions have the culture laboratory connected to the operating room. Since the operating room is sterile and the distance the oocyte must travel is short, there is less risk of contamination. To further insure success it is important to have an animal model of in vitro fertilization occurring simultaneously. Most commonly mice are used. Normal growth and development of the mouse model provides assurance that the system is working well. In addition, all culture media are changed weekly to further reduce the risk of contamination.

EMBRYO TRANSFER

Embryo transfer is perhaps the simplest and most straightforward technical asect of IVF. Yet it is also the most disappointing, as most of the failures of IVF occur at this step. The patient is taken from her hospital room, on her hospital bed, to the operating room. The procedure is performed in the operating room for two reasons, one to insure sterile technique, and two because the culture room is next to the operating room. Antibiotics are routinely given to patients from the time of laparoscopy until two days after the embryo is placed in the uterus. Occasionally a second medication is given to reduce uterine cramping. It is hoped that this will prevent expulsion of the embryo once it has been transferred. In order to benefit from gravity, the women must be properly positioned for this procedure. If her uterus tips backward, she is positioned on her back, If her uterus tips forward, she is positioned with her knees and chest against the bed, as if she were kneeling forward looking under something. A speculum is then placed into the vagina, and the cervix is cleansed with culture medium. A special teflon catheter has been designed for this procedure It is approximately twelve inches long and very thin. The end of the catheter is closed with a small opening on the side of the catheter near the top, through which the embryo is loaded by means of a syringe connected to the other end. The catheter is then threaded through the cervix to the top of the uterus where the embryo is released. The catheter is held in place for one minute and slowly withdrawn along with the speculum. The patient, still on her hospital bed, is taken back to her room where she remains at total bedrest for twelve to twenty-four hours. She is then discharged from the hospital and asked to remain in bed as much as possible for the next twenty-four to forty-eight hours.

SUCCESS RATE AND AVAILABILITY OF IVF

Today more than 100 centers around the world are performing IVF. Since 1978 over 200 living births have occurred as a result of this technique. Around Christmas of 1981 America's first live birth from in vitro fertilization occurred. Most interestingly, Mrs. Brown, mother of the first IVF baby, has borne a second IVF baby. A positive pregnancy test occurs in up to 20 percent of attempts, but a viable child only occurs in approximately 10 percent of the patients treated. In order to place these success rates in perspective, one must recognize that the human reproductive system is very inefficient. Of 100 eggs exposed to potential fertilization only 31 will produce a viable offspring. The other 69 percent will be lost, usually prior to the first missed period. Therefore, the best result that can be anticipated is 31 percent. It is hoped that improvements in fertilization techniques and in embryo growth and transfer will increase the success rates over the next few years. One means of improving the outcome is to reimplant more than one embryo.

With the exception of a single congenital heart defect not genetically related, all of the children born from IVF have been normal and healthy. Originally it was felt that amniocentesis, a procedure whereby a needle is placed into the amniotic fluid of an early pregnancy to see if normal development is occurring, was a necessary procedure in pregnancies resulting from IVF. However, this procedure is not without risk. One totally genetically normal baby was lost in Australia due to an infection that resulted from this procedure. Currently, most doctors feel that should an abnormal pregnancy occur, it would result in a miscarriage just as in the majority of situations where abnormal pregnancy occurs under natural conditions. However, a small percentage of genetic abnormalities occur in nature under natural conditions. For this reason the couple must be given the option to choose whether or not they feel the risk of amniocentesis is worth the potential information that would be gained.

The current success rate with IVF is still relatively low. However, significant advances over the past two to three years have made this procedure a reality. Over the next decade I anticipate that continued advances in this area will improve the outcome to approximate that of nature. I feel that availability will be as widespread in America as it is in the rest of the world.

Ethical Considerations

There has been a considerable amount of opposition to IVF from "right to life" advocates, particularly in the United States. This is surprising when one considers that the procedure is designed to aid nature in the achievement of fertility and in no way destroys life. Some of the objections are based upon erroneous conceptions of the methodology involved and the risk to the mother and potential offspring. Other objections are based upon philosophical points of view, concerning which there are considerable differences of opinion.

Many opponents to IVF persist in objections that are based upon the erroneous information that in the process a number of embryos are formed, that only one is reimplanted, and that the others are discarded. This may have been the original approach of Steptoe and Edwards and in procedures which may still exist in other countries, but it is not the procedure now followed by the majority of centers. If one uses the natural cycle, only one egg is available for fertilization and implantation. Even if one utilizes fertility medications and attains two or more eggs and fertilizes more than one egg, all of these fertilized eggs are reimplanted. The argument against IVF based upon the discarding of embryos is thus invalid.

There are natural concerns, as in any new procedure, about safety for both the mother and the potential offspring. As far as the mother is concerned, laparoscopy is a relatively minor procedure performed routinely for all types of gynecologic indications. Patients often undergo major abdominal surgery for infertility with chances of success not much greater than in this procedure. The risks for the potential offspring have been more difficult to assess. This was more of a problem early in the development of the procedure, but with experience more information has accumulated. What has been of concern has been potential chromosomal damage that would result in the birth of an abnormal child. Animal experience has shown that this procedure does not result in any significant increase in abnormal offspring. Studies of spontaneous human abortuses have indicated that when severe chromosomal damage occurs in early pregnancy, spontaneous abortion will occur in more than 99 percent of the cases. There is no suggestion that the careful handling of the embryo results in any chromosomal damage, but if it did, the chance of an abnormal baby would thus be very rare. Furthermore, it must be remembered that even with natural fertilization, abnormalities do occur in about 3.5 percent of live births. Finally, the ongoing experience with IVF brings about greater and greater confidence. There have been approximately 200 babies born by this procedure. One child was born with congenital heart disease, a condition not caused by chromosomal abnormalities. The remainder are normal, healthy babies. Therefore, the evidence at this time suggests that there is no greater risk of abnormalities than with natural fertilization, and that IVF itself does not cause abnormalities.

Finally, it is impossible to counter arguments based upon philosophical beliefs. One can only hold to one's own beliefs. There are those who object to the procedure because they feel that it brings about creation of life in an unnatural way. To answer these objections that life begins at fertilization, there are those scientists who believe that life is a continuum carried through the chromosome material of both the egg and sperm from generation to generation. Life is always present. There is no particular moment when it begins.

Fertilization in the petri dish should be considered as fertilization taking place in an artificial fallopian tube. It can be considered comparable to an artificial kidney or other artificial organs. The embryo only remains two days in this environment. For the remaining 278 days of growth and development it rests in its mother's womb. One of my patients considered this procedure analogous to a coronary bypass. In her opinion, IVF was simply a "fertility bypass." What is important is that medical science has brought the egg and sperm together in a situation where disease has made it impossible or very unlikely that this union would occur. Without this progress hundreds of thousands of couples will be doomed to childlessness.

"We do not create life in the test tube. Life is already there in the living egg and the living sperm. When some disease prevents them from getting together in the customary way, we merely provide the opportunity for them to come together in a different setting". . . .Patrick Steptoe.

REFERENCES

Biggers, J.D. In vitro fertilization and embryo transfer in human beings. *New England Journal of Medicine 304*:336, 1981.

Edwards, R.G., Steptoe, P.C., & Purdy, J.M. Fertilization and cleavage in *in vitro* preovulatory human oocytes. *Nature 227*:1307, 1970.

Edwards, R.G. Test-tube babies, 1981. *Nature 293:*253, 1981.

Evans, M.I., Mukherjee, A.B., Schulman, J.D. Human *in vitro* fertilization. *Obstetrical and Gynecological Survey 35:*71, 1980.

Evans, M.I., & Dixler, A.O.: Human *in vitro* fertilization—some legal issues. *Journal of the American Medical Association 245:*2324, 1981.

Johnston, I., Lopata, A., Speirs, A., Hoult, I., Kellow, G., & duPlessis, Y. *In vitro* fertilization: The challenge of the eighties. *Fertility and Sterility 36:*699, 1981.

Lopata, A., Johnston, I.W.H., Hoult, I.J., & Speirs, A.I. Pregnancy following intrauterine implantation of an embryo obtained by *in vitro* fertilization of a preovulatory egg. *Fertility and Sterility 33:*117, 1980.

Marsh, F.H., & Self, D.J. *In vitro* fertilization: Moving from theory to therapy. *Hastings Center Report.* June, 1980.

Seibel, M.M., Smith, D.M., Levesque L., Borten, M., & Taymor, M.L. The temporal relationship between the luteinizing hormone surge and human oocyte maturation. *American Journal of Obstetrics and Gynecology.* 142:568, 1982.

BIBLIOGRAPHY

MEDICAL, EDUCATIONAL, AND ORGANIZATIONAL ISSUES MEDICAL MANAGEMENT OF THE INFERTILE COUPLE

FEMALE AND COMBINED INFERTILITY

Behrman, S.J., Kistner, R.S., eds: *Progress in infertility.* Boston: Little Brown & Co., 1975.

Menning, B.E. *Infertility.* A guide for the childless couple. New Jersey: Prentice-Hall, 1977.

Shane, J.M., Schiff, I., & Wilson, E.A. The infertile couple. *Ciba Clinical Symposia:* 28, Number 5, 1976.

Taymor, M.L. *Infertility.* New York: Grune and Stratton, 1978.

MALE INFERTILITY

Amelar, R.D., Dubin, L., & Walsh, P.C. *Male infertility.* Philadelphia: Saunders, 1977.

PREGNANCY LOSS

Borg, S. and Lasker, J. *When pregnancy fails: Families coping with miscarriage, stillbirth and infant death.* Boston: Beacon Press, 1981.

Friedman, R. & Gradstein, B. *Surviving pregnancy loss.* Boston: Little, Brown & Co, 1982.

Health Care

Arms, S. *Immaculate deception.* San Francisco: Houghton Mifflin Co., 1975.

Boston Women's Health Book Collective. *Our bodies, ourselves,* 2nd Edition. New York: Simon and Schuster, 1976.

Burgess, A.W., & Lazare, A. *Community mental health and target populations.* Englewood Cliffs, N.J.: Prentice-Hall, 1976.

Psychiatric and Emotional Aspects of Infertility
General References

Abse, D.W. Psychiatric aspects of human male infertility. *Fertility and Sterility, 17:*133–9. Jan.–Feb. 1966.

Benedek, T., Ham, G.C., Robbins, F.P., & Rubenstein, B.B. Some emotional factors in infertility. *Psychosomatic Medicine, 15:*485. 1953.

Berger, D.M. Psychological assessment of the infertile couple. *Canadian Family Physician, 20:*89, Oct. 1974.

Berger, D.M. The role of the psychiatrist in a reproductive biology clinic. *Fertility and Sterility, 28:*141–5, Feb. 1977.

Bierkens, P.B. Childlessness from the psychological point of view. *Bulletin of the Menninger Clinic. 39*(2):177–82, Mar. 1975.

Bresnick, E.K. Infertility counseling, in *Infertility,* ed. M.L. Taymor, Ch. 15, pp. 94–98, Grune and Stratton, 1978.

Bresnick, E.K. A holistic approach to the treatment of the crisis of infertility. *Journal of Marital and Family Therapy.* Vol. 7, No. 2, April 1981.

Denber, H.C. Psychiatric aspects of infertility. *Journal of Reproductive Medicine 20:*1, 23–9, Jan. 1978.

Drake, T., Buchanan, G., Takaki, N., & Daane, T.A. Unexplained infertility, a reappraisal. *Obstetrics and Gynecology 50:*644, 1977.

Drake, T., & Tredway, D. Spontaneous pregnancy during the infertility evaluation. *Fertility and Sterility 29*(1):36–38, July 1978.

Eisner, B.G. Some psychological differences between fertile and infertile women, *Journal of Clinical Psychology 19:*391, 1963.

Farrer-Meschan, R. Importance of marriage counseling to the infertility investigation. *Obstetrics and Gynecology 38:*316–25, August 1971.

Johnston, D.R. The history of human infertility. *Fertility and Sterility, 14:*261–72, May–June 1963.

Karahasonoglu, A., Barglow, P., & Growe, G. Psychological aspects of infertility. *Journal of Reproductive Medicine, 9:*241, 1972.

Lenton, E.A. et al. Long term followup of the apparently normal couple with a complaint of infertility. *Fertility and Sterility 28*(9): 913–9, Sept., 1977.

Mai, F.M., Munday, R.N., & Rump, E.E. Psychiatric interview comparisons between fertile and infertile couples. *Psychosomatic Medicine 34:*431, 1972.

Mazor, M. The problem of infertility in M. Notman and C. Nadelson, eds. *The woman patient.* Vol. I, Ch. 11 pp. 137–160, New York: Plenum, 1978.

Mazor, M. Barren couples. *Psychology Today,* May 1979.

Mazor, M. Psychosexual problems of the infertile couple. *Medical Aspects of Human Sexuality,* Vol. 14, No. 12, p. 32, Dec. 1980.

McGuire, L.S. Obstetrics and gynecology: Psychologic management of the infertile woman. *Postgraduate Medicine 57*(6):173–6, May 1975.

Menning, B.E. *Infertility: A guide for the childless couple.* Englewood Cliffs, N.J.: Prentice-Hall, 1977.

Menning, B.E. The infertile couple: A plea for advocacy. *Child Welfare* Vol. 54(6), June 1975.

Menning, B.E. The infertile couple, in Burgess A. and Lazare, A., eds., *Community mental health: target populations,* Ch. 7 pp. 104–121, Englewood Cliffs, N.J.: Prentice-Hall, 1976.

Menning, B.E. The emotional needs of infertile couples. *Fertility and Sterility,* Vol. 34, No. 4, p. 313, October 1980.

Mozley, P.D. Psychophysiologic infertility: An overview. *Clinical Obstetrics and Gynecology 19*(2) 407–17, June 1976.

Noyes, R.W., & Chapnick, E.M. Literature on psychology and infertility: A critical analysis. *Fertility and Sterility* 15:543–58, Sept.–Oct. 1964.

Platt, J.J., Ficher, I., & Silver, M.J. Infertile couples: Personality traits and self-ideal concept discrepancies. *Fertility and Sterility* 24(2) 972–976, Dec. 1973.

Wilchins, S.A. The use of group 'rap sessions' in the adjunctive treatment of five infertile females. *Journal of the Medical Society of New Jersey.* 71(12): 951–3, Dec. 1974.

Williams, L.S., & Power, P. The emotional impact of infertility in single women: Some implications for counseling. *Journal of the American Medical Women's Association* 32(5):327–33, Sept. 1977.

INFERTILITY AND SEXUAL FUNCTION

Debrovner, C.H., & Shubin-Stein, R. Sexual problems in the infertile couple, *Medical Aspects of Human Sexuality* Jan. 1975, pp. 140–150.

Debrovner, C.H., and Shubin-Stein, R. Sexual problems associated with infertility. *Medical Aspects of Human Sexuality,* Mar. 1976, pp. 161–162.

Elstein, M. Effect of infertility on psychosexual function. *British Medical Journal,* 3:296, 1975.

Kaufman, S.A. The impact of infertility on the marital and sexual relationship. *Fertility and Sterility* 20:380–3, May–June 1969.

Walker, H.W. Sexual problems and infertility. *Psychosomatics.* 19(8): 477–84, Aug. 1978.

INFERTILITY AND ADOPTION

Andrews, R.G. Adoption and the resolution of infertility. *Fertility and Sterility,* 21:73–6, Jan. 1970.

Arronet, G., Bergquist, C., & Parehl, M. The influence of adoption on subsequent pregnancy in infertile marriages. *International Journal of Fertility.* 19(3):159–162, Mar. 1974.

Kaplan, R.A., & Glass, R.N. Adoption in an infertility clinic. *Connecticut Medicine, 37:*563–5, Nov. 1973.

Renne, D. 'There's always adoption': The infertility problem. *Child Welfare, 56*(7):465–70, July 1977.

Sandler, B. Conception after adoption: A comparison of conception rates. *Fertility and Sterility, 16:*313–33, May–June 1965.

ADULT DEVELOPMENT AND THE LIFE CYCLE

Anthony, E.J., & Benedek, T., eds. *Parenthood: its psychology and psychopathology.* Boston: Little, Brown, 1970.

Erikson, E. *Identity and the life cycle, psychological issues.* Monograph I, International Universities Press, New York, 1959.

Levinson, D., Darrow, C., et al. *The seasons of a man's life.* New York: Knopf, 1978.

Notman, M. Women and mid-life: A different perspective. *Psychiatric Opinion, 15*(9) 15, Sept. 1978.

Ross, J.M. The development of paternal identity: A critical review of the literature of nurturance and generativity; Boys and men. *Journal of the American Psychoanalytic Association 23:*783–817, 1975.

Ross, J.M. Paternal identity: Reflections on the adult crisis and its developmental reverberations, *On sexuality: psychoanalytic observations,* eds. T. Byram Karasu and C.W. Socarides, New York: International Univ. Press, 1979.

INFERTILITY AND PUBLIC POLICY FORMULATION

Dienes, C. Thomas. *Law, politics and birth control.* Chicago: University of Illinois Press, 1972.

Friedson, E. *The profession of medicine: A study of the sociology of applied knowledge.* New York: Dodd, Mead and Co., 1972.

Kass, L. Making babies revisited. *The Public Interest,* No. 54, Winter 1979.

U.S. Public Health Service, Reproductive impairments among current-ly married couples: United States, 1976, *Advance Data.* Public Health Service. No. 55, Jan. 24, 1980.

Westoff, C.F. Marriage and fertility in the developed countries. *Scientific American, 239* (6):51–57, Dec. 1978.

DEMOGRAPHIC ASPECTS OF INFERTILITY

Grant, A. Spontaneous cure rate of various infertility factors, *Australia and New Zealand Journal of Obstetrics and Gynecology, 9:*224, 1969.

Raymont, A., Arronette, G.H., & Arrator, W.S. Review of 500 cases of infertility. *International Journal of Fertility, 14:*141, 1969.

Weir, W.C., & Hendricks, C.H. Reproductive capacity of an infertile population. *Fertility and Sterility. 20:*289, 1969.

ADOPTION

THE MENTAL HEALTH LITERATURE

American Academy of Pediatrics—Committee on Adoption. Identity development in adopted children, *Pediatrics,* 1971, *47:*5, 948–949.

American Civil Liberties Union. Adoptees fight to know who they are, *Civil Liberties,* 1975.

Asch, S.S., & Rubin, L.J. Postpartum reactions: Some unrecognized variations. *American Journal of Psychiatry, 131*(8):870–874, August 1974.

Bodmin, J., Silberstein, R., & Mandell, W. Adopted children brought to child psychiatry clinic. *Archives of General Psychiatry, 9:*451–456, 1963.

Deutsch, H. Adoptive mothers, *The psychology of women. Vol. 2 — motherhood.* New York: Grune and Stratton, 1945.

Fisher, F. *The search for Anna Fisher,* p. 36. Greenwich, CT: Fawcett Crest, 1973.

Frisk, M. Identity problems and confused conceptions of the genetic ego in adopted children during adolescence. *Acta Paedo Psychiatreca, 31:*6–12, 1964,.

Kadushin, A. A follow-up study of children adopted when older: Criteria of success. *American Journal of Orthopsychiatry, 37:*530–539, 1967.

Klaus, M., & Kennell, J. *Maternal-infant bonding.* St. Louis: C.V. Mosby, Co., 1976.

Lawton, J. Jr., & Gross, S. Review of Psychiatric Literature on Adopted Children. *Archives of General Psychiatry 11:*635–644, 1964.

Lifshitz, M., Baum, R., Balgur, I., & Cohen, C. The impact of the social milieu upon the nature of adoptees emotional difficulty. *Journal of Marriage and the Family,* pp. 221–228, February 1975.

Marion, T.S., & Hayes, A. An updated cross-cultural literature review on adoption: Implications for future interventions. *JSAS Catalog of Selected Documents in Psychology,* Vol. 5, Fall 1975.

Marion, T.S., & Hayes, A. Primary prevention in an adoptive parent group: Theoretical considerations. *JSAS Catalog of Selected Documents in Psychology,* Vol. 5, Fall 1975.

Marion, T.S., Hayes, A., & Wacks, J. Coping skills and competence acquisition for adoptive families: A new model. Paper delivered to the annual meeting of the American Association of Psychiatric Services for Children, New Orleans, November 1975.

Nadelson, C. The emotional aftermath of adoption. *American Family Physician, 14*(3):124–127, Sept. 1976.

Offord D., Aponte, M., & Cross, L. Presenting symptomotology of adoptive children. *Archives of General Psychiatry 20:*110–116, 1969.

Pannor, R., Sorosky, A., & Baron, A. The effects of the sealed record in adoption. *American Journal of Psychiatry 133:*900–904, 1976.

Peller, L. About telling the child about his adoption. *Bulletin of the Philadelphia Association of Psychoanalysis, 11:*145–154, 1961.

Peller, L. Further comments on adoption. *Bulletin of the Philadelphia Association of Pshchoanalysis, 13:*1–14, 1963.

Pringle, M.L. Kellmer. *Adoption: Facts and fallacies: A review of research in the United States, Canada and Great Britain between 1948 and 1965.* London: Longmans, Green & Co., Ltd., 1967.

Sants, H. Genealogical bewilderment in children with substitute parents. *Child Adoption, 47*:32–42, 1965.

Schechter, M.D. Observations on adopted children. *Archives of General Psychiatry 3*:21–32, 1960.

Schechter, M., Carlson, P., & Simmache, J. Emotional problems in the adoptee. *Archives of General Psychiatry,* 1964, 10:109–118.

Schechter, M.D. Psychoanalytic theory as it relates to adoption, *Scientific Proceedings,* 695–708, 1966.

Schechter, M.D. About adoptive parents, Ch. 17, Anthony, E.J. and Benedek, T. (eds.), *Parenthood: its psychology and psychopathology.* Boston: Little, Brown, 1970.

Senn, M., & Solnit, A. *Problems in child behavior and development.* Philadelphia: Lea and Febiger, 1968.

Simon, N., & Senturia, A. Adoption and psychiatric illness. *American Journal of Psychiatry,* 1966, 122:858–868.

Sorosky, A., Baron, A., & Pannor, R. The reunion of adoptees and birth relatives. *Journal of Youth and Adolescence, 3*(3):195–206, 1974.

Sorosky, A., Baron, A., & Pannor, R. Identity conflict in adoptees. *American Journal of Orthopsychiatry, 45*(1):18–27, 1975.

Toussieng, P. Thoughts regarding the etiology of psychological difficulties in adoptive children. *Child Welfare,* 59–65, February 1962.

Triseliotis, J. Growing up fostered. *Adoption and Fostering, 94*:11–23, 1978.

Triseliotis, J. *In search of origins.* Boston: Beacon Press, 1975.

Wolfenstein, M. How is mourning possible, R.S. Eissler, et al. (eds.), *The psychonanalytic study of the child,* Vol. 21, pp. 93–123. New York: International Universities Press, 1966.

GENERAL REFERENCES

"Children Without Homes, The Report of the Children's Defense Fund." Can be obtained by sending $5.50 to the Children's Defense Fund, 1520 New Hampshire Ave., N.W., Washington, D.C. 20036.

Kirk, H.D. *Shared fate: a theory of adoption and mental health.* New York: The Free Press, 1964.

Klibanoff, S. and Klibanoff, E. *Let's talk about adoption*. Boston: Little, Brown & Co., 1973.

MacNamara, J. *The adoption advisor*. New York: Hawthorne Books, Inc., 1975.

Martin, C. *Beating the adoption game*. LaJolla, California, Oak Tree Publications Inc., 1980.

Plumez, J.H. *Successful adoption: a guide to finding a child and raising a family*. New York: Harmony Books, 1982.

Van Why, E. *Adoption bibliography and multi-ethnic sourcebook*. Available through NACAC, 250 East Blaine, Riverside, California 92507.

SPECIAL NEEDS ADOPTION

Anderson, D.C. *Children of special value*. New York: St. Martins Press, 1971. In-depth study of children of "special needs" in adoption.

Blank, J.P. *19 steps up the mountain: The story of the DeBolt family*. Philadelphia and New York: J.P. Lipincott Company, 1976.

Kravik, P., ed. *Adopting children with special needs*. Available through NACAC, 250 East Blaine, Riverside, California 92507.

OLDER CHILD ADOPTION

Berman, C. *We take this child*. New York: Doubleday and Co., 1974.

Carney, A. *No more here and there*. Available through NACAC; 250 East Blaine, Riverside, California 92507.

Jewett, C. *Adopting the older child*. Harvard, MA: Harvard Common Press, 1977. Available through NACAC; 250 East Blaine, Riverside, California 92507.

Jewett, C. *Parent's guide to adopting the older child*. Available from Open Door Society of Massachusetts; 600 Washington Street, Boston, MA 02111.

Kadushin, A. *Adopting older children*. New York: Columbia University Press, 1970.

Transracial and International Adoption

De Hartog, J. *The children*. New York: Antheneum, 1969. A look at older child Korean adoption and adjustments.

Doss, H. *The family nobody wanted*. New York: Scholastic Book Services, 1971.

Duling, G. *Adopting Joe; a black Vietnamese child*. Rutland, Vermont: Charles E. Tuttle Company, 1977.

Kramer, B., ed. *The unbroken circle*, 1975, a collection of writings on interracial and international adoption, available from OURS, 3148 Humboldt Ave., South; Minneapolis, Minn. 55408, (over 470 pages).

Ladner, J. *Mixed families*. Garden Press, N.Y.: Anchor Press, 1977. Available through NACAC; 250 East Blaine, Riverside, California 92507.

Margolies, M., & Gruber, R. *They came to stay*. New York: Coward, McCann and Geoghegan, Inc., 1976.

Taylor, M. *Intercountry adoption handbook*. Available from Open Door Society of Massachusetts; 600 Washington Street, Boston, MA 02111.

Adopted Adults and Birthparents

Lifton, B.J. *Lost and found; the adoption experience*. New York: The Dial Press, 1979.

Sorosky, A., Baran, A., & Pannor, R. *The adoption triangle*. Garden City, New York: Anchor Press/Doubleday, 1978.

Triseliotis, J. *In search of origins*. Boston: Beacon Press, 1975.

Books for Children

Bunin, C. and S. *Is that your sister?* New York: Pantheon Books, 1976. Available through NACAC; 250 East Blaine, Riverside, California 92507.

Livingston, C. *Why was I adopted?* Secaucus, New Jersey: Lyle Stuart, Inc., 1978. Available through NACAC; 250 East Blaine, Riverside, California 92507.

Lowry, L. *Find a stranger, say goodbye.* Boston: Houghton Mifflin, 1978.

Miles, M. *Aaron's door.* Boston: Little, Brown and Co., 1978.

Silman, R. *Somebody else's child.* New York: Frederick Warne, 1976.

CHILDFREE LIVING

Bombardieri, M. *The baby decision:* How to make the most important choice of your life. New York: Rawson Associates, Scribners, 1981.

Peck, E. *The baby trap.* New York: B. Geis Association, 1971.

Peck, E., & Senderowitz, J. *Pronatalism: The myth of mom and apple pie.* New York: Thomas Y. Crowell and Co., 1974.

Whelan, E.M. *A baby?. . .maybe.* New York: The Bobbs-Merrill Co., Inc., 1975.

ARTIFICIAL INSEMINATION BY DONOR (AID)

Beck, W.W. Jr. A critical look at the legal, ethical and technical aspects of artificial insemination, *Fertility and Sterility, 27*(1):1–8, Jan. 1976.

Curie-Cohen, M., Luttrell, M.S., & Shapiro, S. Current practice of artificial insemination by donor in the United States, *New England Journal of Medicine,* Vol. 30, No. 11, p. 585–589, March 15, 1979.

David, A., & Avidon, D. Artificial insemination donor: Clinical and psychological aspects, *Fertility and Sterility, 29*(5):528–532, May 1976.

Dixon, R.E., & Buttram, M. Artificial insemination using donor semen: A review of 171 cases, *Fertility and Sterility, 27*(2):130–134, Feb. 1976.

Gilbert, Sarita. Artificial insemination, *The American Journal of Nursing*, February 1976, pp. 259–260.

Shane, J., Schiff, I., & Wilson, E. The infertile couple, *Ciba Clinical Symposia, 28*(5), 1976.

Snowden, R. and Mitchell, G.D., *The artificial family: a consideration of artificial insemination by donor.* London: George Allen and Unwin, 1981.

A Personal Account

Atallah, Lillian. Report from a test-tube baby. *New York Times Magazine.* April 18, 1976, p. 16. Written by an adult who was conceived by AID and has full knowledge of it.

Legal Cases Involving AID

Gursky v. Gursky, 39 Misc. 2d 1083, 242 N.Y.S. 2d 406 (Sup. Ct. 1963).

Orford v. Orford, 49 Ont. L.T. 15, 18, 58 D.L.R. 251, 253-4 (1921).

MacLennan v. MacLennan, [1958] Sess., Cas. 106, [1958] Scots L.T.R. 12 (Sess. Ct. Outer House).

Kusior v. Silver, 54 Cal. 2d 603, 354 P. 2d 657 (1960).

INFERTILITY RELATED TO EXPOSURE TO DES *IN UTERO*

Medical Problems in Daughters

Barnes, A.B., Colton, T., Gundersen, J., Noller, K.L., Tilley, B.C., Strama, T., Townsend, D.E., Hatab, P., & O'Brien, P.C. Fertility and outcome of pregnancy in women exposed *in utero* to diethylstilbestrol, *New England Journal of Medicine*, Vol. 302, No. 11, pp. 609–613, March 13, 1980.

Berger, M.J., & Goldstein, D.P. Reproductive outcome of DES exposed women. Fertility and sterility, *Obstetrics and Gynecology*, Vol. 55, No. 1, pp. 25–27, Jan. 1980.

Goldstein, D.P. Incompetent cervix in offspring exposed to diethylstilbestriol in utero, *Obstetrics and Gynecology*, *52:*73s–75s, 1978.

Koufman, R.H., et al. Upper genital tract changes associated with exposure in utero to diethystilbestriol, *American Journal of Obstetrics and Gynecology*, *128:*51–59, 1977.

MEDICAL PROBLEMS IN SONS

Cosgrove, M., Benton, B., & Henderson, B.E. Male genitourinary abnormalities and maternal diethylstilbestriol, *Journal of Urology*, *117:*220–222, 1977.

Eliasson, R. Analysis of semen, *Progress in infertility*, 2nd Edition, S.J. Behrman and R.W. Kistner, eds. Boston: Little, Brown and Co., pp. 691–713, 1975.

Gill, W.B., Schumacher, G.F.B., & Bibbo, M. Structural and functional abnormalities in the sex organs of male offspring of mothers treated with diethylstilbestrol (DES), *Journal of Reproductive Medicine*, *16:*147–153, 1976.

Gill, W.B., Schumacher, G.F.B., Hubby, M.M., & Blough, R.R. Male genital tract changes in humans following intrauterine exposure to diethylstilbestrol. In Herbst, A.L. and Bern, H.A., *Developmental Effects of Diethylstilbestrol (DES) in Pregnancy*. New York: Thieme-Stratton Inc., 1981.

Henderson, B.E., Benton, B., Cosgrove, M., Baptista, J., Aldrich, J., Townsend, D., Hart, W., & Mack, T.M. Urogenital tract abnormalities in sons of women treated with diethylstilbestrol, *Pediatrics*, *58:*505–507, 1976.

MEDICAL PROBLEMS IN DAUGHTERS AND SONS

Bibbo, M., Gill, W.B., Azizi, F., Blough, R., Fang, V.S., Rosenfield, R.S., Schumacher, G.F.B., Sleeper, K., Sonek, M.G., & Wied, G.L. Follow-up study of male and female offspring of DES-exposed mothers. *Obstetrics and Gynecology, 49:*1–8, 1977.

Dieckmann, W.J., Davis, M.E., Rynkiewicz, L.M., & Pottinger, R.E. Does the administration of diethylstilbestrol during pregnancy have therapeutic value? *American Journal of Obstetrics and Gynecology, 66:*1062–1075, 1953.

McLachlan, J.A., Newbold, R.R., & Bullock, B. Exposed prenatally to diethylstilbestrol, *Science, 190:*991–992, 1975.

Shapiro, S., & Slone, D. The effects of exogenous female hormones on the fetus, *American Journal of Epidemiology,* 1979.

EMOTIONAL ASPECTS OF DES EXPOSURE

Apfel, R.J., & Fisher, S.M. Emotional implications of DES exposure for mothers, daughters, sons and doctors. Presented at the American Psychiatric Association, Chicago, Ill., May, 1979.

Burke, L., Apfel, R.J., Fisher, S., & Shaw, J. Observations on the psychological impact of DES exposure and suggestions on management, *Journal of Reproductive Medicine,* March, 1980.

DES Task Force Report, U.S. Dept. H.E.W., Sept., 1978.

Schwartz, R.W., & Stewart, N.B. Psychological effects of diethylstilbestrol exposure. *Journal of the American Medical Association 237:*252–254, 1977.

Yalon, I.D., Green, R., & Fisk, N. Prenatal exposure to female hormones. Effect on psychosexual development in boys, *Archives of General Psychiatry, 28:*554–561, 1973.

PRENATAL GENETIC DIAGNOSIS

Erbe, R.W. Prenatal diagnosis of inherited disease, *Human health and disease.* P.L. Altman and D.D. Katz, eds. Bethesda, MD.: Federation of America Societies for Experimental Biology, 1977.

Fuchs, F. Genetic amniocentesis, *Scientific American,* Vol. 242, No. 6, pp. 47–53, June 1980.

Miller, W.A., & Erbe, R.W. Prenatal diagnosis of genetic disorders. *Southern Medical Journal, 71:*201–207, 1978.

NICHD National Registry for Amniocentesis Study Group: Midtrimester amniocentesis of Prenatal Diagnosis. Safety and Accuracy. *Journal of the American Medical Association, 236:*1471–1476, 1976.

COUNSELING THE AMNIOCENTESIS PATIENT

Finley, S.C., Varner, P.D., Vinson, P.C., & Finley, W.H. Participants' reaction to amniocentesis and prenatal genetic studies, *Journal of the American Medical Association, 238:*2377–2379, 1977.

Mueller-Heubach, E., Garver, K.L., & Ciocco, A.M. Prenatal diagnosis of trisomy X: its implications for genetic counseling, *American Journal of Obstetrics & Gynecology, 172*(2):211–212, 1977.

Robinson, J., Tennes, K., & Robinson, A. Amniocentesis: its impact on mothers and infants. A one-year follow-up study, *Clinical Genetics, 8:*97–106, 1975.

Sorenson, J., Swazey, J., & Scotch, N., *Reproductive pasts, reproductive futures, genetic counseling and its effectiveness,* Monograph of the March of Dimes Birth Defects Foundation, Vol. 17, No. 4, New York: Alan R. Liss, Inc., 1981.

A PERSONAL ACCOUNT

Boutelle, Ann. *Suspense in pregnancy.* Vogue, September 1978.

IN VITRO FERTILIZATION

Biggers, J.D. In vitro fertilization and embryo transfer in human beings, *New England Journal of Medicine, 304:*336, 1981.

Edwards, R.G., Steptoe, P.C., & Purdy, J.M. Fertilization and cleavage *in vitro* of preovulatory human oocytes, *Nature, 227:*1307, 1970.

Edwards, R.G. Test-tube babies, 1981. *Nature, 293:*253, 1981.

Evans, M.I., Mukherjee, A.B., & Schulman, J.D. Human *in vitro* fertilization, *Obstetrics & Gynecology Survey, 35:*71, 1980.

Evans, M.I., & Dixler, A.O. Human *in vitro* fertilization—some legal issues, *Journal of the American Medical Association 245:*2324, 1981.

Johnston, I., Lopata, A., Speirs, A., Hoult, I., Kellow, G., & duPlessis, Y. *In vitro* fertilization: The challenge of the eighties, *Fertility and Sterility 36:*699, 1981.

Lopata, A., Johnston, I.W.H., Hoult, I.J., & Speirs, A.I. Pregnancy following intrauterine implantation of an embryo obtained by *in vitro* fertilization of a preovulatory egg, *Fertility and Sterility, 33:*117, 1980.

Marsh, F.H., & Self, D.J. *In vitro* fertilization: Moving from theory to therapy. *Hastings Center Report.* June, 1980.

Seibel, M.M., Smith, D.M., Levesque, L., Borten, M., & Taymor, M.L. The temporal relationship between the luteinizing hormone surge and human oocyte maturation, *American Journal of Obstetrics and Gynecology.* In Press.

ORGANIZATIONS AND RESOURCES

Adoption Resource Exchange of North America (ARENA)
67 Irving Place
New York, N.Y. 10003
(212) 254-7410

A clearinghouse of information about adoption in North America, especially in helping find homes for children with "special needs."

American Fertility Society
1801 9th Ave., South
Birmingham, Alabama 35205
(205) 933-7222

It is possible to write or call the Society and make inquiries about the closest medical specialists in infertility.

DES Action National
East Coast:
Long Island Jewish Hillside Medical Center
New Hyde Park, N.Y. 11040
(516) 775-3450

West Coast:
1638-B Haight Street
San Francisco, CA 94117
(415) 621-8032

A national nonprofit organization, with local chapters offering information, referrals, literature, legal information, professional education. For DES daughters, sons, and their parents.

Office of Cancer Communications
National Cancer Institute, Room 10A17
National Institutes of Health
Bethesda, MD 20014

DES pamphlets not limited to cancer are offered.

Families for Children, Inc.
10 Bowling Green
Pointe Claire 720
Quebec, Canada

Resources for several types of international adoptions.

Holt Adoption Program
P.O. Box 2420
Eugene, Oregon 97402

Agency dealing with international adoptions, primarily in South Korea.

National Organization for Nonparents
806 Reistertown Rd.
Baltimore, MD 21208

Organization founded by Ellen Peck that promotes and supports the decision to remain childfree.

NACAC (North American Council on Adoptable Children)
250 East Blaine
Riverside, CA 92507

An affiliation of parent groups in the U.S. and Canada. Membership is $10 per year and includes subscription to ADOPTALK. Other publications are available.

Open Door Society of Massachusetts, Inc.
600 Washington Street
Boston, MA 02111

Parents' group for adoptive parents. Membership is $8 per year and includes bimonthly newsletter. Other publications available.

OURS (Organization for a United Response)
3148 Humboldt Ave., South
Minneapolis, Minn. 55408
(612) 827-5709

Adoptive parent organization with a wealth of experience, especially in international adoptions, and an excellent bi-monthly newsletter filled with adoption information.

Planned Parenthood
  Federation of
  America
810 Seventh Avenue
New York, N.Y. 10019

A source of information
about health care and
doctors.

RESOLVE, INC.
P.O. Box 474
Belmont, MA 02178
(617) 484-2424 (9:00–
  4 P. M. weekdays)

A national, non-profit,
charitable organization
that helps infertile peo-
ple. Services include a
free telephone counsel-
ing service; referral to
medical services or al-
ternatives; support
groups for infertile
people; public educa-
tion; and much litera-
ture.

World Family
  Adoptions, Ltd.
5048 Fairy Chasm Rd.
West Bend, Wisconsin
  53095

International adoption
agency.

INDEX